Jewish Wisdom For Growing Older

Finding Your Grit & Grace Beyond Midlife

Rabbi Dayle A. Friedman, MSW, MA, BCC

16
EasyRead Large

RHYW

Copyright Page from the Original Book

Jewish Wisdom for Growing Older:
Finding Your Grit and Grace Beyond Midlife

2015 Quality Paperback Edition, First Printing

Library of Congress Cataloging-in-Publication Data
Friedman, Dayle A., 1956– author.
Jewish wisdom for growing older : finding your grit and grace beyond midlife / Rabbi Dayle A. Friedman, MSW, MA, BCC.
pages cm
Includes bibliographical references.
ISBN 978-1-58023-819-9 (pbk.)
1. Aging—Religious aspects—Judaism. 2. Older Jews—Care. 3. Older Jews—Religious life. 4. Self-actualization (Psychology) in old age. I. Title.
BM540.A35F76 2015
296.7084'6—c23
2015000952

ISBN 978-1-58023-832-8 (eBook)

10 9 8 7 6 5 4 3 2 1

Manufactured in the United States of America
Cover Design: Jenny Buono
Cover Art: © Yulia von Eisenstein/Shutterstock
Interior Design: Tim Holtz

For People of All Faiths, All Backgrounds
Published by Jewish Lights Publishing
A Division of LongHill Partners, Inc.
Sunset Farm Offices, Route 4, P.O. Box 237
Woodstock, VT 05091
Tel: (802) 457-4000 Fax: (802) 457-4004
www.jewishlights.com

TABLE OF CONTENTS

To my mother, Audrey Friedman Marcus, who demonstrates that one can grow older with vibrant engagement, courage, and a great appetite for fun.

In memory of my beloved sister, Jill Friedman Fixler, whose dignity, grit, and grace as she faced her cruel illness and untimely death will forever inspire me.

In memory of my father, Don Friedman, who taught me about transforming relationships as we grow older.

To be old is a glorious thing when one has not unlearned what it means to begin.

—Martin Buber

[Growing older] is hazardous, but worth the effort.

—Rabbi Everett Gendler

INTRODUCTION

Births Out of Brokenness

Growing Whole as We Grow Older

> The challenge of aging isn't to stay young; it's not only to grow old, but to grow *whole*—to come into your own.
>
> —*Connie Goldman*[1]

What Is Beyond Midlife?

When we are young, we fantasize about what life will be like when we grow up. We try on visions of our futures and happily share them with anyone who will ask. When we get to midlife and look ahead, most of us do not have a similarly clear picture of what we hope for, much less what we expect. We do not know how to propel ourselves into the terrain of later life. Many of us approach this next part of the life cycle with trepidation. We are afraid of the known—the end of this part of life is inevitably death—and of the unknown: How will we fill the days and years? How will we cope with new roles and the loss of old ones? How will we go on when we lose those dear to us?

Those of us approaching this part of our paths now can expect, if we are lucky, to live for several more decades. It is unlikely that we will face unadulterated disability and decline, as many of us fear. It is just as doubtful that we will have only triumphs, adventures, and joys.

It is not possible to break this post-midlife time into neatly demarcated stages. We cannot distinguish "healthy" from "ill" phases, since we may go back and forth between these states. And it is not particularly meaningful to divide the time by chronological age, since you could be eighty-five and playing tennis every day or sixty-four and physically disabled with multiple sclerosis. You could be retired at sixty and enjoying a life of volunteerism or be eighty-six and working full-time. You could be fifty-eight and have school-age kids at home, like me, or seventy-two and becoming a grandparent for the first time. You might be grieving the loss of a longtime partner at sixty-one or falling in love at ninety. It is probably more helpful to see this unfolding as rich, complicated, and challenging.

The journey beyond midlife is strewn with both joys and sorrows. The complex path ahead will include aging, changing, becoming, learning, forgetting, loving, losing, waxing, waning, ailing, healing, teaching, caring, being nurtured, feeling pain, savoring pleasure, doing, being, and dying. It is not a straightforward trip but rather an unfolding path full of twists and turns, of shocking surprises and, if we are open, perhaps unexpected delights. We cannot plan this journey; we simply cannot anticipate when and how our health will challenge us. We cannot prophesy about the future economic environment or how others around us will fare. Even if we have seen others go down this road, we will never be able to anticipate just what will happen or how it will be for us. We need guidance to find our way with resilience, courage, and blessing—to develop grace and grit in facing what lies before us.

Births Out of Brokenness

We can take strength from a teaching by the kabbalistic master Rabbi Isaac Luria. According to Luria, the world we live in, the life we have, was born out of a cosmic shattering *(shever).* God had intended to fill the world with the divine light, but the world could not endure this intense and overwhelming splendor. God contracted the divine presence in order to make room for the world, but in a devastating cosmic accident, the vessels intended to hold God's light shattered.

The light that was abundant and omnipresent was suddenly hidden and dispersed—encased in shards *(kelipot)* of the vessels that had been meant to contain it. So now the Divine is limited and concealed in a world of darkness. In the wake of the cataclysm, we are alive—there is space for us in the world—but we are in darkness. It is up to us human beings to locate and lift up the sparks of light hidden within the shards that surround us. This is the work of repairing the world *(tikkun olam).*

This mystical cosmology turns out to be an apt description of the journey beyond midlife. We are constantly encountering shatterings as we grow older—partings with jobs or roles; disappointments as things don't turn out the way we imagined; health crises; leaving cherished homes or communities to begin again somewhere else. We may feel that the light that illumined our way and gave us joy has left us. When things shatter in our lives, we are, in the words of health and wellness expert Elizabeth Lesser, "broken open,"[2] and in this way we become available to *begin anew,* with the capacity for deeper-than-ever learning.

We are wounded by the shatterings of growing older, and yet if we are alive, we have new opportunities to grow. As the Catholic priest Richard Rohr teaches in his book *Falling Upward,*[3] we can grow into the fullness of our human potential. This opportunity for growth emerges out of the shattering. Actually, later life is a series of births out of brokenness. We might wish to go back, but we are not given that choice. The *only* existential choice is whether we will dwell in the darkness or seek (and lift up) the sparks of light hidden within our new reality. This is what Rabbi Luria called *tikkun*—repair.

My sense is that the whole journey beyond midlife is a mysterious blend of light and dark, wholeness and fragility. I have seen the very oldest old and frailest frail share ecstatic joy and make a profound difference in the world around them. I have also seen people whose outer lives may have changed little felled by a single loss or a change.

We have a chance beyond midlife to become the person we were truly meant to be. We can draw on everything we have experienced so far to contribute to the people around us and the wider world and to find strength and resilience amid challenges.

Prepare Provisions for the Journey

How are we to equip ourselves to be able to seek out—and find—the hidden light amid our experiences beyond midlife? Another ancient teaching gives us a hint. Isaac Abravanel, a medieval Jewish sage, taught that later life has a unique purpose. Once we have passed through midlife, he posited, it is time to "attend to our soul" and to "prepare provisions for the journey." What journey? The journey from now until our last breath. Abravanel suggests that as we grow older, we ought to live differently than we have before. Now, we place our focus on gathering spiritual sustenance for the path ahead. He does not mean that we are to stop all work or creative activity, or even that we must retire at any specific time, but rather that the center of our concern becomes growing deeper and wiser.

This book offers provisions for the journey beyond midlife. If you were setting off for an extended camping trip, you would pack all manner of things to sustain you. You would bring food and water for your body (or tools with which to gather them), clothes and blankets to protect you, and means of making fire to comfort you. In traveling on the path beyond midlife, it's not jerky or trail mix that you will need, but perspective, guidance, and practices. These are the things that will sustain you as you grow older.

Jewish tradition has for millennia approached growing older with a healthy combination of reverence and realism. Judaism offers a storehouse of wisdom through its practices, narratives, and norms; it offers just the kind of inspiration and guidance that can help seekers of all faiths find radiance and resilience as they age. In this book you will have an opportunity to draw from this ancient wisdom in order to lay in provisions—to learn, grow, experiment, and develop approaches to becoming whole in this unprecedented swath of life.

The book begins with exploring shatterings beyond midlife—changes and challenges that we must confront in the journey toward wholeness. The second part of the book offers pathways toward searching for sparks of light—beginning anew in the wake of change, loss, and limits. The third section offers approaches to basking in the light we have found—by living fully and generously. Each chapter includes stories of people I've met and accompanied in my work as a rabbi (details and names have been changed to protect their privacy), teachings from Jewish tradition to frame the dimension of the journey we are discussing, and spiritual practices you can explore to add to your provisions for the journey.

At the end of each chapter, I offer you a blessing to sustain you along the way. You can read these blessings, taking them in as a hope, a gift, for you. Or perhaps you will want to say these blessings for yourself; if so, you can change the wording to the first person ("may I," instead of "may you"). In chapter 15 you will learn more about the power of blessings. You will encounter several different blessing practices to try out as a means of enriching your days. You can read the book from start to finish, or you can dip into a particular chapter at a time when it is most relevant to what you are experiencing. You may want to record your reactions and reflections in a journal you set aside for this purpose. In the appendix, you will find a guide to using this book in a book group or wisdom circle.

Is This Book for You?

This book is for you if you are approaching retirement and imagining what you will do with the rest of your life. This book is for you if you are facing health challenges and realize you cannot maintain the lifestyle you have had until now. The journey of caregiving is a gateway to our own process of aging. This book is for you if you are in midlife, caring for aging parents, and wondering both how to help them and how you will find a way to thrive when it is your time to grow older.

This book is also for you if you work with aging people, as a health-care or social service professional, clergyperson, or chaplain. You may find concepts that will help you hold and heal others and sustain your own spirit.

This book is written from the perspective of Judaism. I believe that the riches of Jewish wisdom and practice can offer sustenance to you regardless of your faith. Perhaps you will read this book and become curious about teachings and practices from your own tradition. Perhaps you'll find the resources in this book speak to you as they are. Feel free, regardless of your background, to take or adapt what is useful and leave what is not.

How I Came to This Journey

I became interested in aging when I was young. When I was a college freshman, I was brought by friends to a Shabbat service at an "old age home," as they called it then. I went with no great enthusiasm but instantly fell in love—with the elders, who were so refreshingly real and vivid—and with the amazing experience of sharing Shabbat across generations. I kept going back for all of my college years.

In a way I have never stopped going back to the rich wellspring of meaning I find in my Jewish tradition and to the fascinating terrain of aging. I have explored this landscape as a rabbi, chaplain, teacher, and spiritual guide. My teachers have been the thousands of elders I have accompanied, from the elders in their eighties and nineties in the nursing home where I served my first congregation, to the "younger old" participants in wisdom circles I facilitate these days. All of them have demonstrated Bette Davis's words, which sit on my desk in a needlepoint made by a ninety-four-year-old congregant: "Old age is not for sissies." I have seen grit and grace, bitterness and brokenness. I have witnessed hearts breaking open and also spirits shutting down in the face of growing older. My desire is to help others grow wiser and more resilient beyond midlife.

This material is no longer distant and exotic for me; it is personal. I am now a fifty-eight-year-old mother, sister, wife, and daughter. In the past several years I have lost many dear ones. I am still sorting this through, even as I have accompanied my beloved sister through terminal illness. My husband and I are parenting teenage and young-adult kids, humbled by the health challenges and little and big life struggles they've faced. And we are growing older. My husband has a Medicare card and I have an AARP card to prove it.

I am looking ahead with curiosity and some worry. I am not old, but I am aging. I wonder how many new big projects I will initiate, how I will cope with losses ahead, what it will feel like to *be* an elder after being *with* elders for so many years. I am seeking provisions for my own journey and am eager to share with you what I have learned through thirty years of accompanying others on this path.

A Blessing for the Path

I hope and pray that this book will help you gain knowledge and provide you with spiritual tools to help you flourish as you grow older. Here is my blessing for all of us on this journey beyond midlife:

> May we grow fruitful as we age
> Ripe and abundant and sage
> Keep our hearts open to all we face
> Present to goodness, even a trace.
> Renew us, let our spirits soar.
> Sustain us, our Rock, for more.
>
> —Psalm 92:15–16 (my translation)

You can listen to a melody for this blessing on my website, Growing Older, http://growingolder.co/spiritual-resources/melodies-chants/may-we-grow-fruitful-as-we-age.

Part I

Facing Shatterings as We Grow Older

1

Seeking Wisdom

Transcending Destructive Ageism

> The crown of glory of old age is attained through righteousness.
>
> —*Proverbs 16:31*

Aging: Better Than the Alternative?

The book of Proverbs describes gray hair as "a crown of glory" of old age (16:31). This "crown of glory" and the longevity it signals are envisioned as a reward for a life well lived. In the classical Jewish imagination, aging is a prize and a source of pride. In fact, there is a Rabbinic teaching that suggests the physical signs of old age came about through a request by the patriarch Abraham. Before Abraham, old age bore no distinctive physical signs. It seems that the very old, vigorous, black-haired Abraham would walk down the street with his young son Isaac, born when he was ninety-nine years old. Passersby could not tell who was the father and who the son. Abraham was upset because he was not receiving the deference he felt was due him as an elder. He therefore prayed to God, "Crown me with wrinkles and gray hair." His prayer was answered and thus was born the scourge of the beauty industry (*Genesis Rabbah* 65:9).

According to Jewish tradition, later life is a rich and beautiful time, and elders are precious treasures worthy of honor. How different is this view from the prevailing youth worship in the culture we live in today. When these texts were written, the average life expectancy was not more than forty years. Now, "aging" can last several decades, perhaps a third of our lifetimes. If you are currently age sixty in the United States, you can expect, on average, to live between twenty and twenty-five more years. Of course, each of us is an individual, not an average; our life expectancy could be much shorter or much longer. Still, it is no longer uncommon to live to our nineties or even past one hundred. How are we to conceive of this huge swath of the life cycle?

Contemporary popular culture offers us extreme visions of existence beyond midlife. On the one hand, we are told by commercials to "just do it"—as we watch ninety-year-olds gleefully bungee jumping or riding off on Harley-Davidsons. You can apparently grow older without changing your level of fitness, energy, or engagement. If anything, the commercials would suggest we might just suddenly become more trim, athletic, and adventurous than we have been until now. Maybe this can go on for decades, maybe forever. We can fulfill every dream, amuse ourselves as we've never done before, and we won't have to worry about a thing.

The "just do it" images exist alongside a diametrically opposed view. We don't have to look far to see abundant images of frail, confused elders apparently dependent and miserable. These portrayals suggest that all we have to look forward to as we age is incontinency and vulnerability—we will be left writhing on the floor, crying, "I've fallen and I can't get up!" We are given to understand that when we are old, we will suddenly and inevitably end up dependent, unable to recognize ourselves in the mirror or find value in our lives.

These simplistic pictures about life's second half—either we magically evade aging's vulnerabilities or we succumb to despair-filled existence—are incomplete and misleading. Both poles point to a deep-seated fear of the latter part of life.

What to Call This Time of Life?

In the many years I have worked in the field of aging, I have noticed something strange: there is *no* term for people in later life that is universally acceptable. "Seniors"—sounds like high school. "Older adults"—why describe someone in a way that is relative to others? "Mature adults"—too many are not. "Elders" (my personal favorite)—unavoidably a reference to aging and thus way too scary. I have thought a great deal about this phenomenon. It seems to me that there are two factors at work here. First, how can we use a single term to refer to a huge swath of life? Just as no one would imagine a label that encompasses both twenty-year-olds and forty-five-year-olds, so too the sixty-year-old and the ninety-year-old may be at very different life stages.

Many contemporary theorists have pointed out that the years between sixty and ninety or a hundred cannot be seen as a single stage or phenomenon. They point to the emergence of a new life phase—*between* adulthood and old age. In *Composing a Further Life,* cultural anthropologist Mary Catherine Bateson describes the impact of the new longevity this way: It's as if you made an addition to your home. The new wing of your home is not stuck on the *end* of your house; rather, it's like an atrium inserted in the middle. Bateson calls the new life phase added by extended longevity "second adulthood," a time of "active wisdom."[1] Social entrepreneur Marc Freedman calls the post-midlife stage "Encore," envisioning our potential for making a contribution to the world around us through paid or volunteer endeavors.[2] Sociologist Sara

Lawrence-Lightfoot calls "the generative space that follows young adulthood and middle age" the "Third Chapter." She suggests that this stage is characterized by "passion, risk, and adventure."[3]

The Scourge of Ageism

There is no doubt that many of the varied experiences of people beyond midlife cannot be captured by conventional concepts of aging. But there is something else going on in our stubborn inability to generate an acceptable label for individuals in later life. No one wants to be called "old" or any of the euphemisms we have for aging because we have ingested a toxic brew of ageism just by living in contemporary society.

My friend Ruth was luxuriating, swimming across a friend's New England pond on a beautiful summer day. At some point, she noticed that she was propelling herself across the water with the breaststroke, not the speedier crawl she had used for years. Yuck, she thought, here I am swimming like an old lady! Ruth, who had recently turned seventy and retired from her respected professional position, suddenly found her delight had turned to disgust.

A friend told me about Ellen, who was musing about her fear of growing old. Time is slipping away, she said. It's like a roll of toilet paper that gets smaller and smaller and turns faster and faster, and then it will be gone and I'll die.

We have swallowed whole what geriatrician Bill Thomas calls the "declinist" view of aging in his rousing call to action, *What Are Old People For? How Elders Will Change the World.*[4] As cultural critic Margaret Morganroth Gullette puts it in her book *Agewise,* "Aging is the new fate worse than death." She writes, "The contemporary shared narrative about later life hammers the inevitable slide into decline, with a better now and a worse later. A much worse later."[5] This declinist view of later life paralyzes and depresses us. The lives of people beyond midlife are profoundly affected by prejudice. Psychologist Todd D. Nelson reports that age prejudice in the United States "is one of the most socially condoned and institutionalized forms of prejudice."[6] This prejudice is evident in employment and housing discrimination, to be sure, but also in the perceived acceptability of mocking and characterizing aging people, as well as in social isolation and invisibility.

Alongside the societal ageism that surrounds us is our own *internalized* ageism. Ruth and Ellen exemplify what happens as we direct ageism toward ourselves. We are unable to actually *see* where we are, what our lives are about. We are terrified that if we are "old," we will be invisible, disgusting, and unlovable. We cannot enjoy the present moment because we are filled with fear about what will come next.

Even if we are blessed with long years of good health, energy, and, we pray, basic economic security, we cannot escape the challenges: people dear to us will die; we may find ourselves coping with serious physical limits; we may be caring for parents or partners struggling with chronic illness; and we face the reality that not all of our dreams will be realized.

No wonder we cannot name the life phase or phases beyond midlife. No wonder it is hard to find a head of undyed gray hair. Of course the aisles of the drugstore are filled with "age-defying" preparations. Rachel Hayes, beauty director of *Cosmopolitan,* argued that the "positive and hopeful" age-defying approach "empowers a woman to have more control over her looks and to try to slow the cruelty of time."[7]

We are understandably drawn to what historian Theodore Rozsak calls the "Senior Follies" in his book *America the Wise*—"the effort to deny or defy aging."[8] Jungian analyst James Hillman wrote in *The Force of Character: And the Lasting Life,* "The main pathology of later years is our idea of later years."[9]

Embracing Complexity

We need a more complex way of holding what for most of us will be a long journey beyond midlife. My teachers, the elders I accompanied as a chaplain through the terrain of frailty and dependency, have taught me that their territory is about more than loss and sadness. They've taught me, and I am suggesting here on their behalf, that we can experience growth, blessing, learning, and contribution, even as we contend with illness or disability.

We desperately need to move beyond the false dichotomy: either we defy age in our second half of life by remaining physically and in every other way vital *or* we are swallowed up by illness or incapacity and languish in what retirement expert Ronald Manheimer has called "the vortex of nothingness."[10]

We can transcend ageism and false dichotomies by *embracing* aging. We can greet the long, complex post-midlife period with curiosity and compassion instead of dread and despair. We start with ourselves and then, fortified by acceptance, we can begin to transform the landscape of growing older for our communities and our world.

PRACTICE: Welcoming Signs of Aging

Place yourself in sight of a mirror. Look carefully at your reflection. What is different from the way you appeared at an earlier time in your life—at twenty-five, thirty-five, or forty-five? Are there wrinkles? Gray hair? Less hair? More of you? Less?

Focus on one manifestation that demonstrates that you are growing older. Try to approach this sign with kindness and affection. Say to yourself:

______ is a sign that I am growing older.

______ is a sign that I have lived a long time.

______ is a sign that I have had rich experiences, both joys and sorrows.

______ is a sign that I have gained understanding through all I've been through.

I am thankful that I have lived this long and hope to live longer still.

Reflect on the experience of trying this practice. If you like, record your reflections in a journal. Do you feel any differently about the signs of aging visible in your appearance?

Seeking Wisdom: Moving toward the Essential

My late mother-in-law, Miriam, had a very fruitful old age. She did not climb mountains or work at a career. She did not travel the world. She did not write books or invent cures. Rather, this amazing woman, who had survived the Warsaw Ghetto and multiple concentration camps before she came to the United States to build a new life and family, was virtually homebound for several years before she died at close to ninety. What she did, in the words of the rabbi who gave her eulogy, was "work the phone." Miriam maintained a regular telephone correspondence with a couple of dozen relatives and friends all over the country. When you spoke to Miriam, she genuinely wanted to hear about your life. She always had not only a kind word but also a piercing insight, usually expressed in the form of a perfectly apt Polish or

Yiddish saying, prefaced with "My mama used to say..." After speaking with Miriam, you saw more clearly or held more lightly whatever was burdening you. The fruit that Miriam bore and boundlessly shared until her dying day was her wisdom.

Rabbi Judah Loew, a sixteenth-century sage, suggests that aging offers a unique opportunity:

> As we age, we become wiser ... as our physical faculties are weakened, our spiritual faculties gain strength, for we acquire the capacity of discernment—spiritual independence, or exalted intellect, which flows from the Holy One. In this way, [the elder] can grasp things that are utterly distinctive. (Maharal on *Pirke Avot* 5:21, my translation)

According to Rabbi Loew, certain capacities are heightened as we grow older. Our bodies may change and face limits, but our souls become unbounded. How is it that we become wiser? Our ability to discern expands. We become able to see clearly, to make distinctions about what is really important, what matters most. We are no longer totally dominated by the perspective of other people and the culture at large. We can hold on to the perspective we have gained from our life experiences. We can forge our own unique insights. Gaining wisdom is, according to Theodore Roszak, "what the elder mind seems especially empowered to do."[11]

What is wisdom? Wisdom is clearly not the same as intelligence, or bright people would not make disastrous choices. Wisdom does not correlate to education, for many wise individuals, like my mother-in-law, have not had access to much, if any, formal learning. Wisdom is rather some ability to draw on experience to gain perspective and insight for the situation or choice one faces.

Psychologists Christopher Peterson and Martin Seligman identify the following elements of wisdom:[12]

- Creativity
- Curiosity
- Open-mindedness
- Love of learning
- Perspective

These dimensions of wisdom seem to be modes of being or character traits of the wise person. Gerontologists James Birren and Lauren Fisher suggest that wisdom involves balancing, on the one hand, the transcending of limitations and, on the other, acceptance of them. They write, "Wisdom is tested by circumstances in which we have to decide what is changeable and what is not."[13] Becoming wise apparently involves finding the sweet spot between determination and surrender.

If wisdom is a way of relating what we have experienced and learned to the reality we face, then how does growing older allow us to hone wisdom? It would be lovely if wisdom would magically appear, but my sense is that we actually have to *work* at becoming wise. Following are a few aspects of the work of forging wisdom as we age.

Reflection

Drawing wisdom out of experience involves actively reflecting on what we have gone through. Wisdom is not a possession, Mary Catherine Bateson suggests, but a *process* born of the willingness to both learn new things and modify earlier learning. Bateson suggests that "[wisdom] *is the fruit of continuing reflection* on encounters over time, a skill at drawing connections and finding similarities, looking for underlying patterns."[14] In other words, we gain wisdom as we challenge ourselves about what it is we think we know, both about our past and about our present.

> Aging, I feel ... is a process that is alive and happening, growing up and getting closer, moving toward the essential.
>
> **—Debra Winger**

The qualities of curiosity and humility help us remain open to this evolving process of gaining perspective. It is when we lack these traits that we risk falling prey to foolishness, according to psychologist Robert

Sternberg. Sternberg suggests that otherwise smart people make hideous mistakes when they believe they are omniscient, omnipotent, or invulnerable. The sense that we do *not* know it all keeps us eager to learn more. Awareness of our limits helps us avoid overstepping our capacity or bounds. We can actually become smarter, or at least wiser, by keeping our egos in check and our eyes and minds open.[15]

Mining Challenges

Growing older inevitably places us in confrontation with loss, limits, change, and disappointment. As unwelcome as these challenges are, it is precisely in facing them that we can deepen our wisdom. For example, Roszak suggests that health crises can be a rite of passage in later life because they impose a "suspension of the ordinary." In the heightened reality of a health crisis, we have an opportunity to be transformed, to enhance our appreciation of the simplest blessings in our lives, and to shift the way we relate to ourselves and others.[16] Of course, this is true with any encounter with vulnerability. We grow wiser by telling the story of our experience, deliberately mining the lessons contained in it. This can be done with other people or on our own, in the form of journaling and self-reflection. This process helps prevent the precious gleanings from painful experience from ebbing away as "normal life" returns.

Seizing the Learning in Every Moment

The Slonimer Rebbe, Rabbi Sholom Noach Berezovsky, a twentieth-century sage, teaches that every day offers each person a particular and unique piece of sacred learning (Torah). No two days are the same, nor is one individual's learning for each day identical with anyone else's. The opportunity for learning from this particular day will not return, he counsels, so we must endeavor to be alert and awake, lest the gift be lost. In this way, we can *come into* our days *(ba bayamim)* like the patriarch Abraham. According to the Slonimer Rebbe, Abraham lived fully each day of his very long life and managed to grasp the wisdom available in every moment. This is the reason, we learn, that Abraham was "old and sated" when he died at 175 years of age.

PRACTICE: The Torah of Your Days

At bedtime, reflect on your day. Ask yourself:

1. What surprised me today?

2. What challenged me today?

3. What disappointed me today?

4. What was the most important moment of my day?

Take a moment to write in a journal about one thing you learned today. This is your personal Torah (sacred teaching). If this piece of Torah leads to an intention about something you would like to do, notice, or experience in the future, note that as well.

Keep up this practice for at least one month. At the end of a month, reread your journal entries. As you take in the accumulated lessons of your days, note whether there is any pattern or theme running through them. Again, ask yourself to form an intention based on this reflection.

A BLESSING

May you open to all the wisdom that will come your way on the path beyond midlife. May you cherish your years and experience and accept change with grace. May you be blessed with strength, and may your heart take courage.

2

One Big Hole

Confronting the Broken heart

Amy lost her beloved fifty-year-old sister, Janie, to cancer. Amy had cared for Janie for several years. Now Amy is the only surviving daughter and caregiver to her parents, who are in their nineties. She nursed her husband through a bout with cancer after Janie died and has ably labored to disseminate Janie's professional legacy. Laid off from the firm she had served for thirty years, Amy has parlayed her professional experience into a busy career as a freelance consultant.

Amy seems buoyant. She is busy, productive, and close to her husband and their young-adult son. But beneath the surface, Amy is struggling. Asked how she was coping after a dear aunt and a beloved mentor died in short order, Amy, now sixty-three, said, "It's like each loss pokes a little hole in you; after a while, they all add up, and there's just a giant gaping hole where your heart used to be."

A Cascade of Losses

When Amy talks about the one big hole that has formed in her heart, she is pointing to the accretion of losses that are a painful aspect of growing older. Aging is much more than loss, but losing is an inevitable part of the journey. As we grow older, we will lose physical capacities. Whether we are faced with the reality that we just cannot do activities we used to cherish (skiing, playing on the floor with grandchildren, gardening) or we are forced to live with significant disability, our bodies will likely change, and not for the better. We may be stripped of roles we have cherished in our professional, communal, or family lives. Perhaps we will find that this particular change brings a loss of status as well. Sadly, we will surely lose precious relationships as dear family members and friends die or move away. Some of us will lose the standard of living that we have attained, and hoped to maintain, as we contend with more limited means due to retirement, economic downturn, or job loss.

These losses of later life have been called the "little deaths" of aging. This image suggests that a small part of us dies with each one of these ephemeral aspects of our lives. In addition, each little death is an intimation of "the big one"—our own mortality. Willingly or not, we are confronted by the impermanence of all that we are and have in this life. How will we face the reality of this cascade of losses?

Can we thrive amid sorrow, or must we succumb to despair?

Naomi: A Biblical Role Model

A biblical story sheds light on the encounter with multiple losses. The book of Ruth opens with Naomi, a woman who has endured unimaginable suffering. Naomi, formerly a denizen of Bethlehem, in the Land of Israel, was forced by famine to decamp to Moab, along with her husband, Elimelech, and two sons, Machlon and Chilion. While in Moab, her sons took local women, Ruth and Orpah, as wives. As the biblical narrative opens, Naomi is returning home to Bethlehem after the untimely deaths of her husband and two sons. She has instructed her daughters-in-law to return to their families, but one, Ruth, insists on accompanying her.

Without her husband and sons, Naomi is shorn of nearly everything she once treasured—love, income, stability, and social station. Once again uprooted, she returns to her former home, but she is not the same. When the local women spy her approaching, they say, "Can this be Naomi?" She replies, "Do not call me Naomi [pleasantness]. Call me Mara [bitterness], for the Almighty has made my lot very bitter. I went away full, and God has brought me back empty. How can you call me Naomi, when God has dealt harshly with me, when the Almighty has brought misfortune upon me!" (Ruth 1:19–21). This once proud woman has utterly succumbed to despair.

Amazingly, Naomi starts over. She ingeniously engineers a marriage for Ruth, thereby protecting her from the physical and economic vulnerability of being a woman on her own. Naomi identifies Boaz, a distant relative with a legal obligation to marry a childless widow of a family member. She instructs Ruth to place herself at the feet of the sleeping Boaz, thereby putting him in a compromising position so that he will feel compelled to fulfill his duty. The scheme works. Boaz marries Ruth and they have a child, Obed, grandfather of King David, and progenitor of the messianic line. Thus Naomi has ensured a promising future, not just for Ruth but for the entire world.

At the end of the story, the townswomen once again address Naomi. They say, "Blessed be the Eternal, who has not withheld a redeemer from you today! May his name be perpetuated in Israel! He will renew your life and sustain your old age; for he is born of your daughter-in-law, who loves you and is better to you than seven sons." Naomi becomes the nursemaid for the baby, and the women declare, "A son is born to Naomi!" (Ruth 4:14–17).

What Keeps Us Going in the Face of Losses?

Naomi has somehow weathered an immense accumulation of losses. She has begun again. She has built a new life and a future. How has she found the strength, courage, and determination to move forward after all she has been through? What can we learn from her about the sources of resiliency for us as we face loss?

Allowing Grief

Naomi certainly does not whitewash the pain of her situation. She gives her sadness vivid expression when she demands to be called *Mara*—bitterness. She names her losses, saying, "I went away full, and God has brought me back empty" (Ruth 1:20). We can easily imagine that Naomi has screamed and wailed plenty. Feeling her pain and giving it expression are very possibly important aspects of her capacity to move forward amid it.

Sandy is a ninety-year-old scientist. Although she is officially retired, she is still involved in publishing her groundbreaking research. Her husband died years ago, as did her daughter. Last year Sandy's beloved granddaughter died suddenly at the age of twenty-six, shortly after Sandy moved from her longtime home to live with her children. Sandy reports, "I wrestle all night. I cry, I ask *why* I had to lose all of them. But when I wake up in the morning, I discover I am excited about the day that lies ahead." Perhaps Sandy's fearlessness in facing the raw pain of her losses creates the space to also find joy in the life she has.

Naomi and Sandy do not resist or deny their grief. They do not pretend that they are undiminished or unscathed. Rather, they give voice to their sorrow, either in conversation or in the quiet of their beds in the darkest moments of night. They are also profoundly engaged with others.

Love

Love is a powerful engine of resiliency. Naomi's love for Ruth provides her with a reason to start over. She simply cannot let her daughter-in-law, who has so lovingly and loyally stuck by her side, die of hunger or be utterly vulnerable to abuse. Naomi manages to thrive amid loss because she has someone to love and someone to care for and because she dedicates herself, through her grandson, to the betterment of the future.

Of course, having friends or family to offer us love when we are bereft is healing. But Naomi teaches us that it is not just receiving love that salves our wounds. *Giving* our own love and caring can be salvific. When our attention is directed toward meeting another's needs, we often find that our own sorrows recede into the background. We might experience this shift in the midst of service. I have heard many volunteers recount that they receive far more than they give when they help needy children, elders, or strangers. We might also find this balm for the spirit as we spend time caring for grandchildren or neighbors.

The enterprise of feeling, and acting, on compassion is actually healing. The Jungian psychoanalyst Polly Young-Eisendrath teaches that compassion is an antidote to suffering and counteracts alienation: "In learning the freedom and wisdom of suffering-with ... [sufferers] discover a new, bigger context in which their lives make sense."[1] Becoming aware of the suffering of others and reaching out to help them can actually salve the wounds of one who suffers.

Young-Eisendrath profiles clinical psychologist Dr. Dan Gottlieb, who lost almost every aspect of life as he knew it when a car accident rendered him a quadriplegic. He often tells the story of the moment early in his recovery that he realized he would be able to go on. Late one night in the hospital, one of his nurses confided in him that she thought about suicide. Dan suggested that they chat after her shift. As he listened to her and offered her his caring and wisdom, Dan could imagine that he could find meaning even if he couldn't use his arms and legs. He began to see that his own pain was enabling him to connect more profoundly with others than he had ever done before.

Our losses can open us up to deep empathy and make us uniquely available to others. Remarkably, as we discover how much love we have, we are empowered to go on.

Savoring Gifts

It might seem paradoxical but along with acknowledging and feeling our losses, finding gratitude for what we *have* can help us reclaim our wholeness. Often as we and our lives are changed by what is no longer here, new blessings crop up—new or deeper relationships with people who show up for us, heightened awareness of beauty, or perhaps a new sense of our own strength. For Naomi, the birth of a grandson was a remarkable and hopeful delight.

Nancy Copeland-Payton, a physician turned chaplain, points out that loss and gift are inextricably linked:

> Life can be walked with gently cupped hands that allow us to let go of outgrown or passing gifts and to receive new ones. There is an art to holding the things of life loosely, letting them flow into and out of our lives without painful grasping.... Again and again, like the repeating cycles of passing seasons, we learn to let go. And in the loss, we receive new gifts.[2]

The awareness of the fleeting nature of all that is precious can awaken us to gratitude for the blessings we experience in each moment. As the Benedictine nun Joan Chittister writes, "It is age that teaches us to enjoy life, to savor every moment of it, to spend our time on what counts, to be present where we are and see it for the first time."[3] This awakening to the treasured aspects of life does not erase tears or eliminate grief. We would not be alive if we did not feel the pain of our losses. We can, though, live with our pain and soften it as we savor the fragile, ephemeral gifts of life.

Jewish tradition teaches us to say blessings, to express appreciation, for all kinds of experiences, positive and negative. As you ponder loss, take time as well to cultivate gratitude. For centuries, the traditional prayer for waking up in the morning known as *Modeh/Modah Ani* (I give thanks) was the first taught to young children. This prayer calls us to cherish the very fact of our continued existence. Whatever threats or dangers you have encountered, you are still here. You get to embrace another day. You might wake up with an aching back, the alarm might go off far too early, but still the invitation of *Modah Ani* is to start the day thankful.

PRACTICE: An Awakening Prayer

- Try saying or singing the *Modeh/Modah Ani* prayer when you wake up in the morning. The words of the prayer are as follows:

Modeh/modah ani lefanecha, melech chai vekayam,

Shehechezarta bi nishmati bechemlah, rabbah emunatecha.

Grateful I arise this day

Eternal God, to You I pray

For my spirit You've renewed in me

Mercifully and steadfastly.[4]

• Make your own *Modeh/Modah Ani* blessing—as you awaken, before you even get out of bed, take a moment to connect with one thing for which you are grateful this morning. Try making the language of the prayer your own, for example: "*Modeh/modah ani lefanecha*—I thank You for [the thing you are acknowledging]." Don't worry too much about the nature of the One you are addressing. Focus instead on how it feels to give thanks, to realize that these blessings you so treasure have come to you without your effort.

• Take several deep breaths. Let the breath fill your belly, your chest, and your throat. With each breath, savor your feeling of gratitude. Let it spread inside you with the breath.

• Notice how your list changes over time—can you get creative in noticing blessings in your life? Notice in what way your days are affected by beginning with gratitude.

A BLESSING

As you face loss, may you open your heart wide. May you feel sorrow in all its depths and still embrace tiny joys. May you take in kindness and savor what you have and have had.

3

The Ultimate Shattering

Embracing Our Mortality

The end of a [person] is to die.

—*Talmud,* Berachot *17a*

On the day before I sit down to write this chapter I learn that my father has apparently entered the final stage of his long journey toward death. Dad has been in a nursing home for the past three years, since he tumbled down the stairs at home. The tragic triad of dementia, heart disease, and diabetes has taken its toll, and he is quite frail. Last week he fell while attempting to get out of his wheelchair and badly injured his hip. He is confined to bed, struggling to breathe, and the hospice people say it won't be long.

I've been preparing for my father's death for three years. I have visited often and said good-bye each time. I am grateful to have had the opportunity to share sweet and healing moments with him; I feel as complete as a person can. Still, I sit down to write this chapter and I find myself ineluctably drawn to every possible distraction. It is Valentine's Day, so I decide to send audio e-cards to every member of my far-flung family. I straighten the house, practice piano, take the dog for a walk. I don't want to write about death. I don't want to think about death. I don't want to face death. Perhaps you feel this way, too. I hope you will read on anyway. As the Torah says, "Be strong and of good courage" (Deuteronomy 31:6, my translation).

We are all aware that we will not live forever. By midlife, we've seen people we love leave this world. And yet ... and yet ... there is some profound way in which we simply do not believe that this will happen to us. Or perhaps we believe it but we cannot accept it. We avoid facing the reality of our mortality. We are afraid. Paradoxically, confronting our own dying can be the opening to living fully for whatever days, months, or years remain. Like a hike up a steep and rocky path that opens up to an unexpectedly magnificent vista, challenging ourselves to acknowledge and face mortality enables us to fill our moments with intensified vividness.

Confronting Our Fears

Rebbe Nachman of Breslov teaches that we live on a very narrow bridge, suspended over the inevitability of death. On this bridge, we walk determinedly forward and don't look down. We avoid contemplating our mortality because we are, most of us, terribly afraid of dying. Our death-denying and death-defying culture magnifies this abhorrence of mortality. Death is shunted aside, cloistered in the world of hospitals and funeral homes. Fantastically lucrative industries sell us myriad products to prevent ourselves from showing our aging, lest we come face-to-face with the ultimate destination of later life. Vast medical resources are invested in futile interventions for patients who have no reasonable hope for survival, because physicians, patients, and families cannot talk about or accept death.

A first step in embracing our human finitude is to get to know our fears, to contemplate the chasm over which the bridge of life hangs. Ask yourself: what scares me about dying?

Common Fears about Dying

Facing the Unknown

None of us knows with certainty what awaits us beyond this world. Elsa, an eighty-year-old widow in the nursing home, stopped me one day in the dining room. "I don't get it," she complained. "My husband has been gone ten years. Not a word. Not a postcard, not even a phone call! Where is he?" Elsa was joking, but there was a serious undercurrent to her jocular remarks. She, who was nearing the end of her life, wondered if death was the end.

Some people I've worked with are convinced that "dead is dead," that the only existence we have is that during our physical life span. It can be terrifying to sense that the self we have developed over our lifetime will simply cease to be. Our roles, our accomplishments, even our love, might just *end.* Particularly if we feel that we have somehow failed to *do* enough or to *be* good enough, this finality is hard to accept.

Jewish tradition offers no dogma on the question of life after death, but it does include a rich array of visions of eternity.[1] Some Jews believe in physical resurrection, at least at the end of days when the world is redeemed. Others have posited the eternality of the soul. Some of these believe in reincarnation *(gilgul nefashot),* while others hold that the soul shines as a part of the eternal flow of life *(tzeror ha-chayim).* Still others affirm what contemporary theologian Rabbi Harold Schulweis called "the immortality of influence."[2] This concept was expressed in the words of the *Union Prayer Book,* which we used in my childhood synagogue: "The departed ... live on earth in the deeds of goodness they have performed, and in the hearts of those who cherish their memories."[3] At best, we can foresee some kind of ongoing existence for ourselves. At the worst, we will endure through the influence we have had while on this earth, even if we will not be aware.

> The whole world is just a narrow bridge, And above all is not to fear at all.
>
> **—Rebbe Nachman of Breslov**

Pain and Indignity

Woody Allen famously said, "I am not afraid of death; I just don't want to be there when it happens." Even if we are sanguine about what will happen *after* death, many of us are profoundly afraid of how we'll get there. We do not want to suffer. We fear pain—we are not at all sure how much we can bear. We may also worry that we will lose our dignity, either in the way we respond to our suffering or in the way that we will be treated when we are dependent on others. We want to retain our power, yet it is highly likely that we will not.

Missing Out

When my children were little, they had a hard time going to bed if we had guests in the house. They would deny they were tired, even as they stifled yawns; they simply didn't want to miss one moment of the fun. For many of us, contemplating death arouses the awareness of all that we love about life. We fear missing out—on juicy experiences, on relationships, on visions yet to be realized. We want to be around to see how it will all turn out. We are afraid that it will hurt to be deprived of all of this.

American author and poet Stephen Levine writes in *A Year to Live,* "It is the fear that makes death seem like a shallow pool viewed from a high cliff."[4] These aspects of dying are surely worthy of trepidation. It is not easy to contemplate losing whatever sense of control we have and whatever it is we have achieved and cherish in this life. Yet evading the reality that we will all die is likely to keep us from living fully as we grow older.

Every Life Is Incomplete

No matter how intentionally we live our lives, we can never complete every task or reach every goal or potential. We learn this lesson quite poignantly from the biblical depiction of Moses. Moses, who dedicated the last third of his life to the project of redeeming his people from slavery, did not manage to reach the Promised Land with them. At the edge of the land he was told that he would die in the wilderness. He would not be allowed to enter the land nor would he witness his people's entrance into the land. Moses argued, cajoled, and begged that he be allowed to enter the land, to see his dream fulfilled, but he was allowed only to glimpse the land from afar.

According to Franz Kafka, Moses is the exemplar of this central truth of human existence:

> He is on the track of Canaan all his life; it is incredible that he should see the land only when he is on the verge of death. This dying vision of it can only be intended to illustrate how incomplete a moment is human life, incomplete because a life like this could last forever and still be nothing but a moment. Moses fails to enter

> Canaan not because his life was too short but because it is a human life.[5]

Like Moses, we will die with one or many aspects of our lives unfulfilled. It is the nature of the human being to continually reach for more than we can grasp. If we have done everything we dreamed of, then we hope to live to see our children or dear ones fulfill their hearts' desires. Eventually we will be called to make peace with this too. When we are very old or very ill, we will come to realize that we will not be adding any more chapters to the book of our lives. We'll find we need to grieve and accept what we didn't accomplish, mend, or experience if we are to have a sense of peace in dying. Meanwhile, keeping our mortality in mind can impel us to live with as much intentionality, goodness, and zest as is humanly possible. We hold the paradox of living vividly, with death in view.

Costs of Evading Death

To avoid our fears of dying, we endeavor to distract ourselves. We pour ourselves into endless work, we seek pleasure excessively, or we become obsessed with maintaining a youthful appearance. As we suppress the deep-down knowledge that all of this can end at any time, we may numb ourselves, cutting ourselves off from our hearts' true longings. On the other hand, when we confront our mortality, taught spiritual innovator Rabbi Zalman Schachter-Shalomi, "what's knocking on our door ... is the agent of the completed self."[6] Facing our own death sets the agenda for the rest of our life. It helps us identify the unfinished business of the past and the callings of the future. Facing dying enables us to grow older with wisdom and intentionality.

Contemplating Dying

A passage from the *Unetaneh Tokef* prayer recited on Rosh Hashanah and Yom Kippur invites us into an extended contemplation of our mortality:

> The origin of the human being is dust, her end is dust. He earns his bread by exertion and is like a broken shard, like dry grass, a withered flower; she is like a passing shadow and a vanishing cloud, like a breeze that blows away and dust that scatters, like a dream that flies away. (High Holy Day liturgy, translated by Reuven Hammer)

> Death is very likely the single best invention of life. It is life's change agent.
>
> —Steve Jobs

The prayer includes stark images of the human lifetime: we are as fleeting as dust that scatters, dry grass that disintegrates, flowers that wither, shadows that pass, breezes that blow, and dreams that fly away. On Yom Kippur, Jews not only contemplate death, we *practice* dying, abstaining for twenty-five hours from food, water, sex, and physical pleasure and dressing in simple white like the shrouds in which Jews are traditionally buried. We are drawn into encounter with our mortality precisely to inspire us to live our limited days as well and fully as we possibly can. With death in mind, we may be brave enough to face our failings and resolve to turn toward our truest, best selves. This does not mean, however, that it is not terrifying to glimpse the finitude of our own lives.

A Talmudic discussion on death features a funny and heartbreaking series of vignettes about famous rabbis and their endeavors to evade the Angel of Death. One rabbi insists that it would be inappropriate for him to be taken while in the act of eating the sacrificial meat. Another argues that it would be undignified for him to come to his end in the marketplace. A third rabbi begs for thirty days' respite so that he can complete his studies; when the Angel of Death later appears at his home, he asks, "What's the hurry?" (Talmud, *Moed Katan* 28a). Clearly, even the greatest sages resist the reality of their lives' finitude.

"And above all is not to fear at all." The word *kelal,* typically translated as "at all," could also mean "everything" or "completely." This translation opens up a valuable understanding. Rebbe Nachman does not actually instruct us not to have fear but rather not to be swallowed up by it. As long as we have breath, we are attached to our life. It would not be reasonable to be unafraid about dying. We can, however, proceed *despite* fear; this is the definition of true courage. We can hold awareness of our mortality without either obsessing or giving up.

PRACTICE: Looking Back, with Compassion

Try this: Sit in a quiet, comfortable place. Give yourself some expansive time. Settle yourself into your spot, notice your feet resting on the floor, your body supported by your chair. Breathe deeply but naturally. Imagine that today is the last day of your life. With compassion and gentleness, ask yourself:

1. What about my life am I proudest of? Is it a professional accomplishment? The way I raised my children? The kindness I showed to my friends? The beauty I never took for granted?

2. What am I grateful for?

3. Which of my past actions do I regret?

4. What experience or adventure am I deeply sorry to have missed?

5. What can I pass on to my children or others who will follow me?

Take some time to reflect on these questions. If you like, jot some notes in a journal. This simple life review affords you a perspective on your life to this point. As you contemplate the blessings and disappointments of your life so far, try to do so with compassion. Give yourself credit for your strivings and your limits, your glories and your flaws. This process of looking back can also help you look ahead to shape your future.

Looking Ahead

As you took a look back on your life, you no doubt became aware of hopes, dreams, and aspirations that you have not yet had a chance to fulfill. Perhaps you have been constrained by the sheer dimensions of your responsibilities to work or family. Perhaps you have been loyal to "shoulds" imposed by parents or community and have sacrificed passions or ambitions. Rabbi Zalman Schachter-Shalomi calls this the "unlived life." He suggests that awareness of our mortality calls us to listen to "the voice of the authentic self," to focus on that which we have left undone or unexplored. If we fail to pick up on these incomplete parts of our lives, he teaches, "our unlived lives are like ringing telephones that we refuse to answer."[7]

> It's all life until death.
>
> **—Grace Paley**

In reviewing your life, you probably also came across regrets and unresolved experiences and relationships. The pain you feel in connection with these memories is a signal that repair *(tikkun)* needs to be done. Coming to a sense of peace, whether through forgiving others who have hurt you or through a process of repentance *(teshuvah)* for your own errors, may form a vitally important part of your future agenda.

Choose Life: Living Each Day Fully

The call of life in the face of death is to be honest, true, and present. The unlived life invites us to embrace, to complete, to reach. Since we know that we will die but cannot know when, should we not make this day, which could be our last, as full and rich as possible? In this precious, finite time we have, we must seize joy and savor it. We must be ourselves for, as an acquaintance's mother taught her, using the words often attributed to the playwright Oscar Wilde, "You might as well be yourself, because everybody else is taken." We must clean up our messes, ask for and grant forgiveness. We must follow our hearts, offer kindness, and do the good we can.

Shema

It is traditional for Jews to say the *Shema* at bedtime: *Shema Yisrael, Adonai Eloheinu, Adonai echad,* "Listen, Israel, the Eternal is our God, the Eternal is One" (Deuteronomy 6:4).

> Rabbi Eliezer taught: "Repent one day before your death." Rabbi Eliezer's disciples asked him: "Do we

know on what day we will die?" "Then all the more reason that we engage in teshuvah [repentance] today lest we die tomorrow! In that manner, all our days will be transformed."

—Talmud, *Shabbat* 153a

It is also traditional for Jews to say the *Shema* as their dying words. Rabbi Zalman Schachter-Shalomi taught that the *Shema* is a way of practicing dying. He hoped, he told me, that by practicing saying *Adonai echad* (the Eternal is One) with his exhalation, when the time came for his last breath he would have these words on his tongue and heart. I am convinced that when he died recently, peacefully in his sleep at age eighty-nine, Reb Zalman's last words were *Adonai echad.*

PRACTICE: Saying Shema

Make yourself comfortable in a sitting position. Inhale naturally through your nose, out through your mouth. As you inhale, say, *Shema Yisrael, Adonai Eloheinu.* As you exhale, say, *Adonai echad.*

As you inhale and exhale to say the *Shema,* imagine this is your last breath. You will no doubt have thoughts about what you will miss from your life and about your regrets. Keep breathing. Bring compassion to yourself. Practice affirming, "I am at one with all life," or "I couldn't be better," or "God is here, and everywhere."

Do this practice every day. Notice how the thoughts and feelings that arise change. You may want to record these thoughts in a journal.

A BLESSING

May you find the courage to see your end while you are still in the midst of your life. May this awareness imbue your days with vividness and wholeness.

4

Finding Wholeness as Our Bodies Break Down

> You may not control all the events that happen to you, but you can decide not to be reduced by them.
>
> —*Maya Angelou*

A friend was once walking down the street with his father, an older man, as they passed a frail older woman being wheeled along in her wheelchair. My friend's father commented, "When I get like that, just shoot me."

This comment is shocking in its starkness but also revealing. We know that aging is bound to include physical decline and illness, yet we fear that reality. Many of us either shut it out of our minds entirely or fervently wish to avoid it altogether. We'd like to reach a ripe old age, enjoy the blessings of extended time, and somehow evade pain, limitation, and weakness.

Intellectually we all know that it is nearly impossible to have long life without physical decline. We have known many elders, probably taken care of parents or other relatives. We have seen it. Although there are "outliers" who make it to eighty or ninety in extreme health and fitness—enough to run marathons or jump out of airplanes—most bodies are eventually vulnerable to illnesses, both chronic and acute. We know this but still we push away this painful awareness. As a friend puts it, our resistance is so strong that as soon as we glimpse the prospect of our own future illness, a curtain of denial comes swooping down.

While we cannot realistically dream of escaping physical limits or suffering as we grow older, we can hope for *wholeness.* We can strive to hold on to life's blessings and to grow spiritually stronger, even as our bodies weaken.

Denying the Decline

A Rabbinic teaching offers an unexpected appraisal of illness's role in aging. The Midrash (Rabbinic exposition) on Genesis suggests that illness came into the world at the request of the patriarch Jacob. How odd that the ancient Rabbis imagined that Jacob would feel bereft were he not to become ill before dying. But Jacob had his reasons: Jacob begged God, saying, "Sovereign of the universe: if a person dies [without having experienced] illness, he [or she] will not [be able to] settle his [or her] affairs with his [her] children" (*Genesis Rabbah* 45:9). So it was that the Torah recounts, "Joseph was told, 'Your father is ill'"

(Genesis 48:1). For the patriarch, separated from his beloved son Joseph for many years, the prospect of dying without his children close at hand, without having a chance to join together for whatever connection might be possible before his earthly end, was unpalatable, to say the least. Illness was a blessing because of what it facilitated for Jacob and his children.

Unlike Jacob, we surely don't ask for physical decline, frailty, or illness, but they come upon most of us nonetheless. Our bodies will not remain as they were. We may discover more of ourselves, with weight that has crept up through midlife, or less, as we lose padding. We may find wrinkles, rolls, baldness, or gray hair. Our endurance and speed are likely to be reduced over time. Our joints may make their presence known with aches or creaks we never felt before. Perhaps a friend or relative will point out that our hearing is not what it was, and we'll have to consider overcoming our resistance to getting hearing aids. All of these are relatively benign and expected physical sides of aging, but when we are relatively well and mobile, we feel, "This is not supposed to happen."

A friend in his mid-sixties was invited to be a substitute player in a neighborhood softball game. He enjoyed taking part in the sport he had long loved, but he tore a muscle doing so. Although the tear will heal, he has reluctantly concluded that he really cannot play anymore. My friend feels real sadness.

His grief foreshadows the grief we will all feel when we face physical challenges that will not get better.

We can and should care for our bodies and maintain our health. We may well have decades of flourishing health, unfettered by pain or illness. If we live long enough, however, our lives will be transformed by chronic illnesses such as diabetes or heart disease or acute illnesses such as cancer or strokes. We are understandably afraid of becoming less well, less able, more limited. Our distress is increased by our repulsion at signs of decline or weakness.

Shifting Our Relationship to Our Bodies

Dr. Diane Reibel, a teacher of mindfulness meditation, asked students in a class I took: When is a rose most beautiful? When it is a bud, all potential, not yet wholly developed or visible? When it is in full bloom, lush with fullness? Or when it is shedding petals, leaving behind reminders of the beauty it once displayed? She invited us to contemplate roses in these various stages. At first I was drawn to the rose in full bloom. I felt it was perfect, rich, complete. It wasn't difficult to see the loveliness of the bud because glancing at it brought with it anticipation of opening to come. The dried rose was much harder to appreciate. I felt sad that its glory was behind it. As I continued to gaze upon the withered petals, I came to glimpse with pleasure the way in which they carried within them all of the rose's story. Without judgment about finitude and frailty, even the dying rose can be treasured. Its shriveling petals carry within them not just the intimation of death but also the memory of their earlier bloom. This realization involved a learning process, a growing toward acceptance.

Just as we can grow to appreciate the preciousness of each stage of the rose, we can come—with effort—to greater peace with our aging bodies. This path toward wholeness involves letting go of the notion that we can forever stay the same. The Fountain of Youth has never been found, despite centuries of searching, whether for a geographical locale or an herb or medicine. Praying that things should not change is a form of idolatry, for we are investing our faith in the impossible.

So in the absence of the magical formula to restore our bodies to the way they once were (or the way we *wish* they had been!), our task is to begin to love our bodies as they are. The spiritual teacher Ram Dass, who suffered a devastating stroke in his sixties, works to greet each pain or physical discomfort with tender compassion, saying, "Ah, so, even this."[1] Perhaps we too can welcome sensations of our bodies with kindness and curiosity. We can look at ourselves in the mirror without bemoaning the changes aging has wrought.

We can try contemplative practice to help us be with a pain or soreness, opening to what exactly the experience is like instead of bracing ourselves against it. This is not to say that we don't do whatever is in our power and seek whatever resources we can obtain to alleviate pain, only that we work to develop a gentler attitude toward our bodies when they are hurting. We are letting go, as much as we can, of defining ourselves based on our bodies' state of being.

We are more than our bodies, and what Reb Zalman Schachter-Shalomi called the "organ recital" of kvetches about our aches and pains does not help us. What may help us is to let go of anger at ourselves, or at aging itself, and honor our bodies for doing as best they can under the circumstances. This letting go may need to happen again and again as our bodies and abilities continue to change. It may help us as well to turn our attention toward others who are suffering, to use our own experience of pain to develop empathy and connection. Brenda, a friend who is in her seventies, has suffered a series of falls and broken bones requiring stays in rehabilitation. She says, "Now I feel a sense of community with others who are disabled or ill. Where I once felt separate, now when I see someone in a wheelchair or using a walker, I feel kinship and compassion."

Living with Limits

We live in a culture that lionizes activity, productivity, and independence. Many of us judge ourselves as lacking if we are no longer doing as much as we once did, whether physically or intellectually. We have accepted the notion that our worth is determined by our level of activity or by what we generate. In contrast, Jewish tradition teaches that our worth is not conditioned on any external measure. We humans are ultimately worthy simply because we are beings created in the divine image.

The Talmud tells of a conversation between a very old sage, Rabbi Shimon ben Halafta, and his lifelong friend and teacher, Rabbi Yehudah ha-Nasi. Rabbi Yehudah asked his friend, "Why did you not come to visit us on the festival, as your parents used to visit my parents?" Rabbi Shimon dolefully answered, "The boulders have grown [seem] tall, that which is near has become [seems] distant, two have turned into three [I need a cane], and the peacemaker of the house has ceased [I am no longer sexually potent]" (Talmud, *Shabbat* 152a). Rabbi Shimon has apparently realistically appraised his physical constraints. What he is basically telling his beloved colleague is, "It is too much for me."

For Rabbi Shimon, slowing down is merely responding to the reality of physical limitations, not a moral failure. Perhaps we can even find a hidden benefit in slowing down. As Ram Dass observes, limits and fatigue "may ... be a message to attend to the moment—to be with it ... to taste it ... to embrace it, a way of making us take time, finally, to tend to what's here now."[2] Psalm 34:9 suggests, "Taste and see how good the Eternal is; happy is the one who takes refuge in God." Instead of rushing to the next thing on our calendar, slowing down may allow us to savor the goodness in each moment of our day.

Jay, a university professor in his sixties, embodies a remarkable balance between acceptance and striving. He resists being defined by his physical challenges. Still, he submits to them as needed and honors the care his body needs to be able to do what it can do, given a chronic illness that severely limits his activities. He says that he spends about half of his life on his illness and tries to find fullness in the other half. For example, on a day when he spends an hour studying with a colleague, the remainder will be filled with four doctor's appointments. Jay says that sometimes he overdoes it and has to pay the price by resting more afterward, and sometimes he misses things he would dearly like to do. He says, "I get very involved in lots of different activities that feed my soul, that all of me engages in ... I'm really there when I'm there, fully." He is inspired by elders he has known and is aware that he is more frail than many of them. He appreciates their courage in getting out of bed, in not giving up. He is in awe of their courage to face every day knowing that it isn't going to get better.

Healing versus Curing

What can we hope for when our bodies decline or fail as we grow older? We would love to be returned to the way that we once were, to "get better." Some ailments do get resolved. A hip repaired may restore mobility to an extent that is almost better than before. Pneumonia might lay us low for weeks but eventually leave without a trace. But many chronic conditions we confront as we grow older will not allow recovery. So what can we hope for? We can hope for *healing.* In the *Mi Sheberach,* the Jewish prayer for healing, we pray for healing into wholeness, healing for the spirit and healing for the body *(refuah shelemah, refuat ha-nefesh urfuat ha-guf).* We can hope for the capacity to feel whole even when the body that carries us is broken. We can aspire to empathy for others who suffer. We can hope for comfort and dignity. We can hope for connection to others who care about us. And we can hope for *shalom,* being at peace with life as it is.

Ella was a tiny, lively woman in the nursing home where I served as chaplain. She had a swallowing difficulty and couldn't eat full meals, so she came to the synagogue on Shabbat attached to a feeding tube, which was plugged into the electrical outlet during services. One Friday evening I came upon Ella delicately unwrapping a little foil-wrapped packet she had brought in her purse. She treated this task with incredible care, and I wondered what treasure was inside. When it was open, Ella took out a small square of chocolate and carefully broke off a tiny piece. She ate it very slowly, with great relish. Ella explained, "You see, I have to take this medicine, which leaves me with a very bitter taste in my mouth, but sometimes I can take it away with a bit of chocolate. Life is like that ... there's a lot of bitter medicine to take, but if you're really lucky, you'll have some sweet chocolate to lessen the bitterness."

As our bodies experience the illness and decline that are normal elements of aging, we can strive to expand our field of vision—remaining awake to the present moment but also seeing beyond this moment and beyond ourselves.

PRACTICE: Loving Your Body

This practice is a contemplative approach to physical experience. This may be unfamiliar to you and perhaps even intimidating. The most important thing to know is that there is no "perfect" way to do it. It is an invitation to be where you are, to inhabit and notice your experience, moment by moment. If you become distracted or feel resistant, try to bring your attention back, gently and with kindness.

Sit or lie in a comfortable position. Breathe normally, paying attention to where you feel yourself inhale and exhale—your throat, your nostrils, your chest, or your belly. Spend a few minutes just noticing the breath. Then direct your attention to each part of your body—your head, face, chest, belly, buttocks, thighs, calves, feet, shoulders, arms, hands.

Notice any discomfort you are feeling in each part of your body, and see if you can learn more about the sensation—is it constant or intermittent, is it hot or cold, does it throb or course? Send very gentle, loving thoughts to each place of pain. See if you can soften or release tightening or tension you feel.

Notice also what does not hurt, savor the absence of pain, and give thanks for that.

If you like, recite this version of a prayer traditionally recited each day in the morning worship service:

Blessed are You, Eternal One, who has formed human beings in wisdom, creating within us a network of organs, vessels, bones, and muscles. I give thanks for this marvelous and fragile body, which makes it possible for me to exist on this earth. I am grateful for all that works in my body. I pray for resilience and the strength to cope when I feel pain. Help me to be whole and to accept limits. Blessed are You, wondrous Healer.

A BLESSING

May you embrace your aging body. May you accept the physical signs of your longevity. May you find comfort for your pain, healing for your spirit, and may you grow toward wholeness with what is.

5

Wandering in the Wilderness

Caring for Our Fragile Dear Ones

Susan, an accomplished professional, is sixty-five. She has looked forward to her husband's retirement, when they would have more time to travel, enjoy their second home, and just relax. Her husband, Mark, has retired, but how different this time is from what she'd imagined. Mark is in his sixth year of battling a degenerative disease, and their beloved toddler grandson is being treated for an aggressive cancer. Susan is doing everything she can to support Mark. She is quietly aching but valiantly trying to keep up the contours of their lives and an upbeat mien amid his steadily eroding health. The effort to maintain appearances—for Mark and for their friends—is stressful as well. Susan travels every few weeks to care for her grandchildren so that their parents can focus on the sick grandson. When friends compliment her on how amazing she is, she thinks, "You should only see me cry in the middle of the night."

Former first lady Rosalynn Carter often cites a well-known adage in the field of family caregiving: "There are only four kinds of people in the world—those who have been caregivers, those who are currently caregivers, those who will be caregivers, and those who will need caregivers."[1] Carter boldly reminds us that caregiving is a universal and unavoidable experience. As we ourselves grow older, we will almost inevitably be called to care for parents, partners, siblings, and friends. The caregiving role will likely be profoundly challenging; it will also begin our preparation for our own aging, as it will place us in intimate relationship with aging. We will learn from the examples of those we care for, positive and negative, about how to cope with dependency, frailty, and dying. We will confront our own fears and very possibly discover strengths we didn't know we had.

As I write this, I am in the midst of caring for my father, who is at the end stages of dementia, heart disease, and diabetes, and my sister, who is contending with a terminal blood cancer. They are both two thousand miles away from the home I share with my husband and two youngest children. Caregiving is not an abstraction for me; I am living this tender and gut-wrenching piece of growing older. I draw on my own experience in framing questions, if not answers, to the dilemmas of caring.

Caring for a person close to us is both provocative and perplexing. As in the wilderness through which the Jewish people wandered for forty years after the Exodus from Egypt, there are few landmarks in the terrain of caregiving, and there is no map. There is vulnerability and sometimes deprivation. We may be stretched beyond our limits—of physical strength, of emotional equilibrium, of finances.

Guilt: What Is "Enough"?

Busy with her own life and work, Sandra, a prominent attorney, pushes herself to the limit, visiting, schlepping, and arranging care for her increasingly frail parents. At work, Sandra knows how to measure success, and she easily gauges how much effort a task requires. Regarding caretaking, she says in despair, "This is not something you can succeed at. No matter how creative I am, how much money I throw at it, how dedicated I am, they don't get better, they just get sicker and needier, and one day, sooner rather than later, they'll die."

When we care for a parent or partner who is chronically ill or disabled, it is hard to know when enough is enough. We can never do for our parents what they did for us. We cannot give them life, and we cannot take care of their every need, both because their needs can be complex and ongoing and because we must juggle multiple, competing obligations.

Lee's ninety-six-year-old father, Sol, fell in the nursing home and needed to go to the hospital to have a cut on his head stitched. It happened that Lee's husband, Morrie, had been hospitalized for a heart attack, and her brother, Lou, died after a long illness on the very same day. Lee had to figure out where to go first: To the hospital with Morrie? To the emergency room with Sol? To the funeral home to make arrangements for Lou's burial?

Lee's story is dramatic but illustrative of the many ways we can be pulled when we are in the midst of caring for our dear ones. Often there is no easy way to be or to give "enough." Of course, we may sometimes—or often—feel guilty. We feel guilty when we need to leave our parent's side to go to a meeting, when we can't stand the idea of going back to the nursing home to visit an in-law, when we resent the demands placed on us, and when, like Sandra, nothing we can do will make it better for our dear one.

Disorienting Shifts in Relationships

Sandy, a seventy-eight-year-old woman, was on vacation with her husband, Stan, when he suddenly became acutely ill. Stan was on a respirator in the hospital for several weeks and only then able to return home. He gradually regained his strength and resumed his activities. For Sandy, though, this dramatic experience felt "as if a cyclone passed through our lives." Life resumed within its normal contours, but a residue of trauma remained. She is not quite sure how to assimilate what happened.

One of the very perplexing aspects of caregiving's impact on relationships is the way our roles change when we take care of the other. It is common to feel a sense of loss or anger, whether it is because our mother can no longer offer her sage advice, or because a partner is not available to manage finances, or because a spouse doesn't feel like a lover when we are changing his or her diaper and bedclothes. We can feel simultaneously called to care for our loved one *and* resentful at the costs of the caregiving on our budget, time, energy, and emotions.

Caregiving can raise powerful dilemmas. What do we owe our parent or care partner, and how does that fit with what we owe our spouse or children, our job? What medical treatments are justified for a loved one at the end of life, and which are unnecessarily burdensome? How do we simultaneously respect the dignity of the care partner and ensure his or her safety and well-being? How do we respect our own limits—perhaps also a feature of our aging—while still being responsible to the person in our care?

Coping with Caregiving's Isolation

Despite the ubiquity of caregiving, those of us who care for others often feel that we are sojourning alone through the wilderness. The demands of caregiving—on top of work, household, and other family responsibilities—may take us away from social relationships and activities. Those around us may have no idea what burdens we are carrying. Even if we are around other people, we may find it difficult to talk about our caregiving challenges. We fear that others won't understand our struggles or feelings.

Our sense of isolation can be exacerbated by conflict within the family over caregiving issues. Often the caregiver who is most nearby has a very different understanding of the loved one's needs and capacities than do siblings or relatives who live farther away, who may see that individual only sporadically. Long-distance relatives' love and concern may be expressed as criticism of the primary caregiver's judgment. Long-standing tensions may rise to the surface. Sadly, instead of supporting one another in the painful confrontation with limits and suffering, family members may be caught in conflict and misunderstanding.

Caregiving can be relentless, particularly when the person in our care is coping with chronic, long-term illnesses, such as dementia. (For more on dementia, see chapter 6.) With all of the compelling demands we as caregivers face, it is easy to forget about our own needs. We may be neglecting health-promoting behavior, such as eating healthy food and exercising. We may forgo involvements that would "refill our cup," feeling that we are not entitled to the scarce resources of our own time and attention.

Sustenance in the Wilderness

The terrain of caregiving can feel barren, like the wilderness the Israelites encountered once they left bondage in Egypt. What can provide sustenance in a harsh surround? For the Jewish people, sustenance came from three key things:

- The pillar of cloud and the pillar of fire that guided them from one place to the next by day and night
- The portable sanctuary *(mishkan)* and the sacrifices offered, which sanctified all kinds of life experiences
- The community of Israel

These three sources of sustenance can support us in the wilderness of family caregiving.

The Pillars of Fire and Cloud: Wisdom

As they wandered in the wilderness, the Israelites had no idea which way to go. There were no guideposts around them. There were, however, divine signs to help them as they moved forward. According to the Torah, they were guided by day by a pillar of cloud and by night by a pillar of fire. For caregivers, the values embedded in Jewish tradition provide an always available source of orientation amid the swirl of decisions and dilemmas that surround us. Within the texts and stories of the tradition are core values that can ground and direct us.

For example, the great Rabbinic sage Hillel teaches, "If I am not for myself, who will be for me? If I am only for myself, what am I? And if not now, when?" (*Pirke Avot* 1:14). This deceptively simple teaching is a wonderful shorthand guide for the caregiver. "If I am not for myself, who will be for me?" The caregiver, according to this teaching, *must* attend to his or her own well-being. No one else can do this. Implicitly, the text suggests, if I do not nourish myself, I will be unable to care for anyone else. This first direction is counterintuitive. One woman who was caring for her aging parents told me, "I hate it when people ask me what I'm doing to take care of myself. I don't have time!" Yet Hillel's teaching demands that we put ourselves on the "to do" list—for the sake of those we care for and for our own sake.

"If I am only for myself, what am I?" The balancing perspective for caregivers comes from the second part of Hillel's wisdom. We are required to attend to ourselves, but ultimately, we are meant to be there for others. We are fulfilling our human potential when we offer compassion and support to the people around us. I have seen many caregivers surprised and delighted by the wellsprings of patience or sheer physical endurance that have become available to them as they meet unforeseen challenges. One daughter told me that her monthly visits to care for her mother, who was in the advanced stages of Alzheimer's disease and no longer able to speak, healed the pain she had felt over a lifetime of receiving judgment and criticism from her mother. "All of that hurt has just melted away," she told me.

A remarkable feature of caring for another is the way in which we often find more resources within ourselves than we knew we had. We do not go through a course in preparation for becoming a caregiver, and we never know when the responsibility will be thrust upon us. It may come on gradually, or it may emerge in a sudden crisis. We find ourselves taking on tasks we never imagined we could handle, whether it is managing complex finances or providing intimate personal care. We discover that we are now the responsible one and that we are competent to handle what we must. In caring for another, we may come into ourselves more fully, tapping unexpected strengths and resilience.

"If not now, when?" Hillel teaches us the incalculable preciousness of the present moment. As caregivers, we need, in each moment, to discern what is most important right now. There may be three, or seven, tasks simultaneously calling us, but we can only do one thing right now. We cannot put off the most important one. And perhaps the most essential thing is not any instrumental task, not a phone call or a bill, but *being there,* if we are able, with the person in our care. The moment may not come again. We're called to tolerate frustration and exhaustion and show up with as much tenderness as we can muster.

My father was never a great driver, but with the onset of dementia and mobility issues his driving became alarming. He would park the car and forget where it was. He could not turn his head around to see what or who might be coming as he merged into traffic. He had several accidents in quick succession. My brother, Glen, and I agreed that he was not safe behind the wheel. I tried to get Dad's doctor to get Dad's license revoked, but the physician told me he could only do so if Dad brought up the subject of driving. On a visit home, Glen and I had a conversation with our stepmother. "Dad really shouldn't be driving," we said. "You tell him," Jeannie said. "OK," we answered. "How about now?"

Suddenly we were sitting around the kitchen table with Dad, and I was thinking, "How did I get into this position? There must be someone else whose job this is!" But I realized that it was up to me and that the moment was now. I said, "Dad, we love you and we want you to be safe, and we want other people we don't even know to be safe. Dad, you can't drive anymore."

"I only drive short distances," he said.

"You can't be sure of being safe, even for one block," we countered.

"You guys are ganging up on me."

"Yes we are, because we care about you."

"I want a driver," he said.

"OK, we'll arrange for someone to drive you places you want to go."

"Oh, all right."

Dad did indeed get help with rides to ease his sense of loss of independence, and all of us were greatly relieved to have acted to avert disaster.

Sometimes we realize we must act and must do so immediately. As my family found, the values highlighted in Hillel's teaching and those reflected in the vast treasure trove of Jewish text and tradition, like the pillars of cloud and fire that appeared to our ancestors, can offer direction and help caregivers discern the path.

The Mishkan: Sanctuary in Place and Time

During their four rootless decades, the Israelites found holiness and sustenance in the sanctuary they constructed and carried with them. In the sanctuary, they were able to connect to the Divine in the midst of their failings, in moments of gratitude, and in their quest for healing and well-being. They marked sacred moments in the cycle of the week, the month, and the year. They joined together, and they reached out.

Jewish spiritual practices can support caregivers on the journey in our day as well. Prayer enables us to bring the language of holiness and blessing to our spiritual distress. Many people who have grown up as Jews are not familiar or comfortable with spontaneous prayer. There, is, however, a deep and long tradition of prayer offered in the moment by an individual.

Rebbe Nachman of Breslov, a brilliant Hasidic sage, suggested the practice of *hitbodedut,* spending time alone "talking to God." He urged that the prayers be said in our own language, with our own words, simply expressing whatever we are feeling and desiring. Even if all we can utter is a simple word or phrase, such as "help me," that, too, can bring connection.

The practice of talking to God may seem strange or forbidding. We might feel silly addressing the Divine when we aren't even sure what we believe in. Rebbe Nachman taught that feeling distant from God or doubting God need not be obstacles, for that too can be shared in prayer. My experience in trying this practice has been remarkable. Overcoming my self-consciousness about it has allowed me to feel comforted and connected in ways that I would never have anticipated. I feel less alone with my troubles, and as my late mother-in-law, Miriam, would say, it's always good to speak what's in your heart *(oysreden dem hartz).*

Prayer, sacred moments such as Shabbat and holidays, and ritual are the spiritual tools of the Jewish tradition. Like the sanctuary, they can provide uplift and grounding, perspective and consolation as we wander in the wilderness of caregiving. Marking the cycles of time—of the week, from Shabbat to Shabbat; of the month, from Rosh Chodesh to Rosh Chodesh; of the year, through the holiday cycle—gives significance to each moment. We are connected to past and future. We are lifted out of the muck of the mundane, even for a moment, into the shining sublime. In the annual holiday cycle, we find our emotional states reflected and shared, as we discover that there is room for joy as on Sukkot, for silliness as on Purim, as well as for grief and loss as on Tisha B'Av.

Kehillah: Community

Caregiving is often invisible—the people we work with or live near have no way of knowing that we race at lunchtime to the nursing home to pick up Mom's laundry or that we spent our vacation with a brother undergoing chemo. We may have no one with whom to share the stress, grief, and confusion we feel.

When the Israelites built the portable sanctuary they carried through the wilderness, God instructed them, "Let them make Me a sanctuary that I may dwell among them" (Exodus 25:8). It is hard to miss the surprising aspect of this order. The result of joining together to construct the holy space is not that God will dwell within *it,* but rather that the Divine will be found in the midst of the people. The message here is that we can find grounding, inspiration, and support when we are in a barren place in our lives by being in relationships, in community.

Many of us have great difficulty expressing vulnerability, asking for or receiving help (see chapter 9). If God is to be found in community, then allowing others to help us can be a path to holiness. We learn from the experience of the Israelites that we transcend the narrow confines of the self when we live in connection, so we need to resist the urge to isolate ourselves when we are caring for our dear ones. When we are in the wilderness of caregiving, accepting help can be a sign of strength, of wholeness, whether it is allowing someone to "spell" us so we can get out, inviting someone to do an errand, or unburdening our hearts by talking about our sorrow.

PRACTICE: Hitbodedut—Talking to God

Experiment with the *hitbodedut* practice. Set aside five or ten minutes several times a week. You can do this in a comfortable, quiet space in your home or on a walk outside. You will want to be alone and undisturbed.

1. Speak to God. Address God by any name you like. Some of the innumerable divine names in Jewish tradition are: Holy One, Source of life, Rock, King, *Shechinah* (feminine divine presence), Father, Wellspring, Eternal One.

2. Say whatever you are thinking or feeling. If what you are feeling is embarrassed, say that. If you are feeling doubt that God even exists, say that too. Speak of your sorrow, or your gratitude, or your exhaustion.

3. Take a few moments of silence afterward just to notice. What was it like to talk to God? How do you feel? Is there any sensation you noticed in your body?

4. Try this practice for a few weeks, just to experience it fully. If you find it nourishing, continue; if not, acknowledge yourself for courage and determination in this spiritual experiment.

A BLESSING

May you who sojourn in the wilderness of caregiving find direction, grounding, and solace as you companion your dear one(s). May you be sustained by the Source of compassion and life itself in this daunting, but sacred terrain.

6

Making Sense of Dementia's Brokenness

Ask your friends and neighbors what illness frightens them more than any other. I'll bet that nine out of ten will name Alzheimer's disease. We dread and avoid diseases of memory loss and those who live with them.

But we are unlikely to successfully evade this experience. Dementia currently affects about four million Americans; this number is expected to rise to fourteen million by 2050. According to current estimates, about 10 percent of those over sixty-five and 50 percent of those over eighty-five have dementia. Dementia will touch us—if we are lucky enough to be spared personally, we are still likely to encounter it in our parents, partners, or friends—and our fear of it colors our perspective on our own aging.

The term "dementia" is often equated with Alzheimer's disease, but in reality Alzheimer's disease is one of a number of related disorders featuring progressive impairment in judgment, thinking, and memory, and sometimes changes in mood, personality, and behavior. Dementia can last for many years; it is sometimes broken down into early, middle, and late stages. The early stage is characterized by loss of short-term memory and mild confusion; the middle stage includes more dramatic confusion and loss of memory and judgment and also often includes incontinence; the late stage involves nearly total deterioration of physical functioning. Eventually, the person with dementia may lose the ability to eat, speak, and walk.

Educator, scholar, and artist Anne Basting, in her daring challenge to conventional conceptions of dementia, *Forget Memory,* outlines some of the myriad fears we associate with dementia, including:

- Fear of being a burden
- Fear of the unknown
- Fear of losing control
- Fear of being violated
- Fear of a meaningless existence

Basting argues persuasively that we need to *transcend* our fears of dementia. She urges us to enter the world of dementia and develop a more complex set of stories and images to reframe and transform dementia. We need to be empowered to open our hearts and minds to a reality more complex than that suggested by the "fear machine."[1]

As a rabbi, chaplain, and spiritual guide to elders and their families, I have accompanied countless individuals as they faced the challenges and losses of dementia—some with courage, some with despair; some with rage, some with dignity. Here are some of the individuals I met as they were living with dementia:

- Mr. Shapiro, a retired pharmacist, was always impeccably dressed in a suit and tie when he lived at the nursing home. He often stopped me when I passed by to ask, "Do you ever get headaches?" I replied that I did quite often get headaches. "Would you like to learn how to get rid of them?" "Sure." Mr. Shapiro showed me that by rubbing my forehead with my thumb and index finger, I could reduce the pain of the headache. Though he did not remember our encounters when next we met, I understood that this man was a helper and a healer, and he was striving to continue to be who he was.

- I met Shirley as I entered her nursing home floor. Obviously distraught, she was near tears. She asked me to help her. "I must find my way home. I'm very late, and my mother is waiting for me. She'll be so worried."

- Rose was an Eastern European woman with quite advanced dementia. She could no longer speak but she could sing, and sing she did, all day and all night. She had an amazing ability to take up any melody you started, in any genre—Broadway, folk, liturgical, klezmer. She didn't sing the words, only "la, la" with great gusto. Teenage volunteers in the nursing home adored being with Rose. They lovingly called her "the la la lady" and competed to sit next to her in the synagogue.

- Sylvia was always brought to Shabbat services on her nursing home floor. She would sit slumped over in her recliner wheelchair all through the entire service; it was not clear if she was asleep or awake. When we sang the *Shema,* the central affirmation of Jewish faith, Sylvia would invariably open her eyes and murmur the words.

Through these experiences as well as perspectives gleaned from Jewish wisdom, I have sought ways to find meaning in the face of dementia. When we have a deeper understanding of the journey of our parents, partners, or friends living with dementia, we may be less afraid and more compassionate as we contemplate the possibility that we may someday have dementia.

Sojourning in the Wilderness: The Experience of the Person Living with Dementia

What is it like to live with dementia? Is it merely a journey of suffering? Can we even know? I cannot say definitively, since I haven't been there. But I have witnessed and reflected upon this experience as I walked alongside those living with it.

One way to conceive of dementia is as a wilderness *(midbar).* We have explored the image of a wilderness in the context of family caregiving. For the Israelites, the forty years of sojourning in the wilderness after their liberation from slavery were mysterious and difficult. They wandered with few markers toward an unknown destination. They could not sustain themselves without divine help. They were vulnerable to unsympathetic people they met along the way and to the harsh realities of nature. They could not return to Egypt, the place of their memories, and they could not imagine what lay ahead.

Perhaps people with dementia experience their lives as a kind of wilderness. Losing memory is the hallmark of their condition. So that you will not be paralyzed by fear and stop reading, I want to assure you that this memory loss is not the same as your constantly losing keys, forgetting the name of that colleague you always enjoy running into at professional conferences, or even searching for the word that is on the tip of your tongue. Annoying though it is, this memory loss is *not* symptomatic of dementia; it is what gerontologists call "benign forgetfulness," and it is rampant beyond midlife.

In contrast, the person with dementia experiences *progressive* loss of memory. Initially, short-term memory fades; eventually, nearly all memory becomes inaccessible. The awareness of this loss is most acute in the early phase of dementia, and it often causes depression or agitation. Losing our memory means losing our connection to pieces of ourselves and, over time, significant aspects of our connections to those who have shared our lives.

In *Agewise,* a wonderfully challenging critique on contemporary ageism, cultural critic Margaret Morganroth Gullette recounts some of her ninety-two-year-old mother's remarks about her memory challenges:

- What I don't remember is an abyss.
- I am an absentee.
- My memory is my worst enemy and my best friend.[2]

When you cannot remember the past and cannot conceive of the future, what you are left with is the present moment. Being present in and aware of the moment at hand can bring joy if the moment is positive but despair if it is not. In that moment of wilderness, nothing else is imaginable.

The wilderness in which the Israelites wandered held places of beauty and moments of amazing power. This is also true for the wilderness of dementia. While memory and other faculties may fade, many people experience an unabated capacity for joy and love, at least until the final stages of the disease. People with dementia sometimes have an especially keen appreciation for life's goodness. For example, my friend Irene described a sublime afternoon spent sitting with her father as they wordlessly watched the falling autumn leaves from the lounge of his nursing home. The two of them were completely absorbed in nature's drama. They had no need for words or action.

When short-term memory fails, the world around you can offer many surprises. Therapist Rita Bresnahan notes:

> And [my mother] is constantly surprised—by flowers that have been in her room for days, or by visitors who just step out of the room for a while. "Oh," she exclaims, smiling broadly at their return, delighted to see them as if they have just come.[3]

In the Creation prayer *(Yotzer Or)* in the traditional Jewish morning worship service, we praise the Eternal for "renewing in goodness each day the work of creation." The one for whom a familiar, beloved person or object repeatedly presents a surprise is living the words of the Creation prayer. In this experience of surprised delight, each moment seems new. The person with dementia may experience what the rest of us are too busy to notice: each moment is a gift and not to be taken for granted.

Unfortunately, the person living with dementia can also suffer dehumanizing treatment by others. In his book *Dementia Reconsidered,* the revolutionary theorist Tom Kitwood decries depersonalizing and malignant responses such as disempowerment, infantilization, and objectification.[4] These dehumanizing responses are rampant in eldercare settings. There are extreme examples, such as a staff member telling an elder who asks to be taken to the bathroom, "Honey, you know you've got a Depends on—just go ahead and pee in it." But there are also more insidious manifestations in the ways people address elders. Perhaps the retired physician doesn't want to be called "sweetie," nor does the homemaker necessarily want to be told how "darling" she looks. Every time caregivers speak about an elder as if they are not present, the elder's dignity is assaulted. Each approach by someone who begins pushing a wheelchair without addressing the person in it is a diminution of their personhood.

The experience of wandering in the wilderness of dementia is made harsher by the negative context that surrounds it. Just as the Israelites were sometimes at the mercy of hostile others in the wilderness, so too those with dementia are vulnerable to attacks on their dignity through dehumanizing treatment. Conversely, the suffering of the person with dementia can be eased by love, respect, and tenderness. As we contemplate the possibility that we will one day have dementia, we can hope that we will be surrounded by love and dignity, so that we will be able to open to the moment with trust.

Loving the Stranger: Shifting Identities, Shifting Roles

When our beloved Grammy Anne suddenly became extremely impaired, unable to sensibly converse and captivated by frightening delusions, my sister, Jill, cared for her with great devotion. Yet, Jill sadly remarked, "This is not Grammy. The person we loved is gone." Encountering dementia in a person we love raises painful questions about what it is that makes us ourselves—now and as we age. If I cannot do the things I have always loved, if I no longer remember my beloveds' names, if I am now disconnected from the events and ideas around me, am I still "me"? If not, who or what am I?

As my family discovered, it can be wrenching to relate to someone you love whose personality has been distorted by dementia. Often the change is negative, as when a distinguished woman disinhibited by dementia suddenly shouts profanities she would never have dreamed of uttering. Sometimes, though, the change can be positive, as I learned when I met the family of Rose, the woman who loved to sing. "You must enjoy her so much," I said. "We do," her daughter said, "especially since she was not always like this. She was tough to live with!" I have met many adult children who found healing and peace in caring for a once-hostile, tough parent who has become softer or more accessible as they live with dementia.

Loving a person with dementia means facing a long, slow farewell, losing your dear one a little bit at a time. You experience the loss anew every time you see the person you love and note again how different they are from the way they used to be. This is an ongoing bereavement but one without routine social or spiritual acknowledgment or support.

Caring for the person with dementia poses a confusing and demanding task. Dementia almost always brings a painful realignment of roles. The direction of power and dependency may shift. There may be weighty new responsibilities and knotty dilemmas. We may find our patience supremely challenged; we might not mind repeating the latest family news twice in a visit, but we might well be annoyed when our parent repeats the same story four times in a single conversation in what seems like an endlessly repeating loop. We may find ourselves consumed by rage at a partner who is suddenly incapable of performing roles we've counted on.

Rita Bresnahan suggests that *acceptance* is a key part of the task in caring for a loved one with dementia. It is so painful to surrender to our inability to fix the inexorable fading of the one we love. "More than anything," she writes, "I need to accept Mom where she is—and accept my own limitations as well. I once heard another caregiver explain to a fellow elevator-rider, 'There is nothing I can do for him, and I am doing it.'"[5]

We might think about the family caregiver's spiritual challenge in terms of the oft-stated biblical command to love the stranger. We must treat the stranger with care, "for you know the soul of the stranger" (Exodus 23:9, my translation). The stranger before you is the very person you have known and loved for all these years. In the confrontation with dementia, you are asked: Can you love this so familiar and yet totally strange person before you? Can you let go of the expectation that the person will behave or appear as she used to, and appreciate her for who she is now? In loving the stranger, can you learn from this person and her journey?

It is a supreme challenge to love the stranger. But we are called to do just that. This challenge of being with a loved one with dementia can go on for years or even decades. It can be truly heroic to experience impatience, grief, and frustration and still compassionately do what needs to be done. Perhaps we can begin to make our peace with dementia, so that should we experience this illness, we will bring compassion toward ourselves and those around us.

Seeing as God Sees: The Divine Image Endures

The biblical creation narrative tells us that God created humanity in God's own image (*betzelem Elohim;* Genesis 1:27). Religion scholar Stephen Sapp suggests that our task in approaching a person with dementia is "to see as God sees."[6] I believe that God sees the *tzelem* in the person with dementia, the divine spark within them that is made in God's image. I am convinced that the *tzelem* is not defined by cognition or capacity. Amid all the changes of dementia, the *tzelem* remains; it is our very humanity. If we are always living in God's image, then perhaps we need to question the assumption that the person with dementia is always suffering or living on a lower plane of existence.

According to Jewish tradition, God remembers *for* us, even when we can't. In the moving words of the *Zichronot* (remembrance) prayers from the High Holy Day liturgy, "Thus says the Eternal, I remembered for you the kindness of your youth, the love of your wedding day, how you followed Me into the wilderness." Even when we are mired in the moment, bereft of all perspective on our lives, God sees more, in boundless compassion. God holds *all* of who we've been. We may forget, but God does not. God "remembers for eternity all of the forgotten ones ... there is no forgetfulness before Your throne of glory."

We are always whole in God's eyes. Knowing this, we can hope to turn this divine sight toward ourselves as we become frail in body or mind.

What to Do? A Path for the Caregiver

In relating to people with dementia, our role is to emulate God, to seek the *tzelem.* We need to remind ourselves that even when the *tzelem* is not apparent, it is there. The image of God somehow resides in the person who is disoriented, regressed, or even unresponsive.

Remember for Them

We can emulate God by remembering *for* those who cannot remember for themselves. We can connect them to memory. As Anne Basting observes, memory is not just the province of the individual but rather "a relational process."[7]

Here is a powerful example from the Talmud. A sage named Rav Yosef bar Chiya was nicknamed "Sinai." So masterful was his command of the laws of the Torah it seemed as if he had heard them directly from God at Mount Sinai (Talmud, *Berachot* 64a). Rav Yosef became ill and suffered major memory loss. In the midst of complex legal discussions, Rav Yosef would repeatedly say, "I have never heard this tradition." His disciple, Abaye, would gently remind Rav Yosef of his own teaching: "You yourself taught this tradition to us, and it was in connection with the following that you told us" (Talmud, *Eruvin* 10a). In reminding his teacher of his own wisdom, Abaye upheld another of Rabbi Yosef's teachings:

> Rabbi Yosef teaches that the tablets [of the law] and the broken tablets [that Moses shattered upon discovering the Golden Calf] are both kept in the Ark. From here we learn that a scholar who has involuntarily forgotten his learning should not be treated disdainfully. (Talmud, *Menachot* 99a)

Abaye connects Rav Yosef not only to his memory but also to his very identity and worth. We can support friends and dear ones with dementia by reminiscing with them and by holding in our memory all that they have been and done in the past.

Respond to the Tzelem

Our challenge is to address the divine within individuals with dementia. As Rita Bresnahan writes:

> It is not *Mom* who must remember who *I* am. Rather, it is *I* who must remember who *my mother* is. Who she truly is. Not merely "an Alzheimer's patient." Nor merely "my mother." It is up to me to [continue to be] ... keenly aware of her spirit, honoring her soul-essence. Meeting her with caring and love and respect in that sacred place of wholeness which nothing can diminish.[8]

One way we can relate to the divine aspect of a person with dementia is through ritual. Lighting candles for Shabbat, celebrating a birthday, or maintaining a cherished family tradition connects to the *tzelem.* Symbol, song, and holy times touch the part that is still whole within the person. This is what happened to Sylvia, who found connection through the familiar words, melody, and message of the *Shema.* Through ritual, the moment is elevated. The individual is acknowledged as more than patient or care recipient. She is a person living in sacred time. Ritual, along with innumerable activities and experiences particular to this person, enables him or her to be in what psychologist Susan McFadden and Pastor John McFadden call the "joy zone" in their beautiful book *Aging Together.*[9]

"I Will Be with You": Accompanying the Person with Dementia

Susan McFadden and Pastor John McFadden suggest that the experience of dementia can be eased by traveling the dementia road together as friends, family, and community.[10] The most important gift we can bring the person with dementia is simply to be with them. Through our presence, we are able to accompany them through the wilderness. Alzheimer's sufferer and author Diana Friel McGowin eloquently states the urgent need as she reflects on her own experience with dementia:

> Without someone to walk this labyrinth by my side, without the touch of a fellow traveler who truly understands my need of self-worth, how can I endure the rest of this uncharted journey? I thirst today for understanding, a tender touch and healing laughter.[11]

Accompanying the person with dementia requires curiosity, inviting him or her to be your teacher. This teaching happens at levels beyond words and surface conversation. We may need to search agitated behavior or garbled speech to unearth the profound concerns the person is trying to communicate. When Shirley tells us she needs to go home to her mother, she is offering profound insight into the enduring mother-daughter bond. When we acknowledge and validate the emotions reflected in apparently "unreal" content, we can reach and honor the confused individual. We will learn much if we open ourselves to our dear one with dementia. Mr. Shapiro, the pharmacist, taught me not only how to relieve a headache but also how to retain one's essential goodness amid change and brokenness. As Margaret Morganroth Gullette says, "The trick for everyone is to be willing to find out what is left—or emerging—rather than what is gone."[12]

In accompanying loved ones with dementia, we may encounter "magic moments," when a person who seems generally quite confused may suddenly speak or connect with great clarity and profundity.

Anna was a feisty, fun-loving woman who had formed many close friendships with other elders in the home in the years she lived there. Only when she passed age one hundred and painfully fractured a hip did she begin to be confused. One day as she reclined in her wheelchair, Anna moaned, saying over and over, "Oy, mama, oy, mama." I sat down next to Anna and took her hand. "You're thinking a lot about your mother, aren't you, Anna?" Anna turned to me and said, "It's always Mom in the end."

Anna could not have said what day of the week it was, and she probably did not remember me. Yet somehow Anna knew what really counted. She realized that she was near the end of her life. She was aware that she longed for the comfort of her mother, and she believed she would soon be joining her.

Ultimately, dementia is a mystery. If we can find the courage to walk alongside those who journey in this wilderness, we too will be transformed. As we learn from those we accompany that they are more than intellect, more than memory, even more than cognition, we learn that we are, too. We learn to value ourselves for our very essence.

PRACTICE: Treasuring Your Divine Soul

Find a quiet spot. Adjust your body so that you are as comfortable as possible. Breathe naturally, noticing the breath entering and exiting your body. When you are grounded in your seat, say to yourself the following phrase: "When I have dementia...." Notice how you feel when you say this, and complete the phrase if you are able. You will probably become aware of hopes as well as fears. Try to hold both with gentleness.

Now say or sing this phrase from the traditional morning prayers: *Elohai neshamah shenatata bi tehorah hi,* "My God, the soul You have given me is pure." Repeat the phrase for a few minutes. Allow yourself to feel holiness and wholeness within yourself. Treasure your divine soul, which is not dependent on memory or on thinking.

A BLESSING

In the awesome and mysterious confrontation with dementia, may you remain connected to the One whose compassion is boundless, who remembers you, and who remembers the covenant that binds you in eternal love. May you bring that compassionate connection to all your relationships.

Part II

Searching for the Sparks

Beginning Again (and Again)

7

Softening to Reality

Finding Sweetness amid Suffering

Behold, it is the truth You desire;
Help me to understand its deepest wisdom.

—Psalm 51:8

My sister, Jill, died of bone marrow cancer at sixty-one. She had known of her diagnosis for thirteen years before she became actively ill. During the four years that she was ill, she was remarkably clear-eyed about what lay ahead. She never for a moment doubted that this sickness would kill her. She pursued treatment to palliate the ravages of the cancer but never fooled herself into hoping that she could survive an incurable ailment.

For the first two years, even as she underwent a series of chemotherapy regimens, Jill continued to work hard and creatively, traveling frequently and building her consulting business. She did not divulge her illness to clients or colleagues. She kept up the contours of her life *despite* her illness—until she couldn't. After she got very sick on a road trip, she concluded that it was time to work only from home.

And when her energy became more limited, she reluctantly decided to sell her business.

One thing that kept Jill going was looking forward to travel. She and her husband, Peter, had planned every detail of a trip to visit their son and daughter-in-law in Israel. They had anxiously anticipated this journey for years. As the date approached, however, Jill had to acknowledge that her strength was too diminished to be able to make the trip and, with great sadness, they canceled. This happened several more times in the ensuing year and a half.

Watching Jill undergo this series of dashed hopes was painful. I felt as if precious pieces of her life were being successively stripped away from her. She was deeply disappointed with each loss. Yet she did not dwell in the place of regret. She said over and over, "It is what it is." She counted her blessings, focusing on gratitude rather than on disillusionment. She delighted in visits from relatives and colleagues from near and far. She reconnected with old friends and deepened her connections with newer ones.

Jill said her illness was not a death sentence but a life sentence. She courageously faced a devastating reality, and heroically squeezed unimaginable goodness out of the last years of her life.

My sister's terrible illness and tragic death make me wonder: how are we to endure the inevitable suffering that will come our way sooner or later as we grow older? The Baal Shem Tov, the founder of Hasidism, outlines three dimensions of responding to suffering in a way that can ultimately prove redemptive: yielding to the darkness *(hachna'ah),* discerning sparks of light *(havdalah),* and wresting sweetness *(hamtakah).*

Yielding to the Darkness

In responding to suffering, the first, immense step is to accept reality. A great Hasidic sage, the Gerer Rebbe, teaches in his commentary *Sefat Emet* (Language of Truth) that even in moments of darkness we can connect to the vital divine power hidden within us by "submitting ourselves before truth" (1:246). We can stiffen and resist the truth of our lives, or we can soften to it. This is not easy or even intuitive—I would certainly prefer to run away from darkness. I guess I am attached to the illusion of control, and I balk at the idea of submitting myself to anything.

Nonetheless, my work with aging people has dramatically demonstrated to me that we are *not* in control; much of what life brings us is not up to us. As we grow older, we face so many unwelcome realities: we lose our dearest companions; we may find new limits on our energy; we will most likely encounter physical frailty; friends or family members may disappoint us; roles that we cherished may evaporate; we may need assistance for tasks we once managed independently.

But denial and resistance may be our reflexive response. "I can still do that." "I don't need help." When we resist painful reality, we add to our suffering (and often to that of the people around us). How many families have struggled when an elder who, like my dad, clearly was no longer capable but insisted on continuing to drive? How many baby boomers have avoided thinking about growing older and thus failed to save money for retirement? As the Buddhist teacher Pema Chödrön writes in her book *The Places That Scare You: A Guide to Fearlessness in Difficult Times,* "Never underestimate our inclination to bolt when we hurt."[1]

This business of yielding to unwelcome reality is so hard. It is natural, reflexive, to deny, to stiffen. When you pull a muscle in your back, your body responds with alarm. Your body attempts to protect the hurt, raw place by hardening around it. You want to make sure that nothing can get to that vulnerable place and injure it further. But a strange thing happens. Instead of feeling better, now you are not only sore but also stiff. You find you have trouble bending, turning, and eventually moving at all. You want to take to your bed; you pray that this will all just pass. Surprisingly, you should do anything *but* this. Stretch, move gently, your doctor tells you, and you will heal. This is yielding.

Discerning the Sparks

The Baal Shem Tov suggests that the second dimension in responding to suffering is discerning sparks of light amid the darkness that surrounds us. I imagine this as a spiritual/emotional parallel to the phenomenon of our eyes adjusting to a darkened room and being able to make out shapes or tiny fragments of light.

To soften to reality, we need to allow ourselves to feel hurt and grief. In this yielding to *what is,* we are liberated from the burden of resisting. We might just find ourselves able to perceive and pursue new possibilities. Scholar and teacher Rabbi Burt Jacobson understands this phase as distinguishing the "voice of the spirit ... the call to freedom, meaning, and joy."[2] Once we know the terrain of our sadness and we can let go of resisting it, we can begin to open ourselves to growth.

Dr. Bill Thomas, a trailblazing advocate for changing the culture of aging, suggests in his book *What Are Old People For? How Elders Will Save the World* that we need to embrace aging in order to live into the potential of elderhood. He decries "the tyranny of still"[3]—the demand that we should *still* do and be the way we used to be, whether it is *still* running five miles a day at age ninety, or *still* working sixty hours a week at age eighty, or *still* making a holiday dinner for twenty-five people at age seventy-five. Thomas is not opposed to any of these activities per se but rather urges us to acknowledge and accept change. He calls us to consider new roles and dimensions of our lives, including departing from busyness and allowing for *being* and reflection. Letting go of "still" and instead looking hard for the sources of light in our current reality is our task now. Maybe we will begin to develop new interests, notice the presence of friends and family, or perhaps simply cry out in prayer.

Wresting Sweetness

Once we have allowed ourselves to dwell in darkness and we have opened our eyes wide to sparks of light within it, the Baal Shem Tov teaches that we are ready for wresting some sweetness out of a bitter experience. It is interesting that the Baal Shem Tov changes his metaphor from darkness-light to bitterness-sweetness. Ultimately, he hints, what we can hope for is to harvest something of sweetness, something redemptive out of our most anguishing life experiences. Rabbi Burt Jacobson suggests that this sweetness can be seen as dispelling the darkness.

It is vital to note that the Baal Shem Tov is certainly not whitewashing the agony of suffering. He himself was orphaned as a young child, his first wife died, and he grew up in an atmosphere of deprivation and violence against Jews. This is not a Pollyannish denial of suffering's sting. Rather, the sage boldly reminds us that even the most wrenching agony may also contain goodness if we are able to be open to it. We may, like Jill, grow closer to those who love us or find our faith deepened. Perhaps we will learn from our suffering and be able to share that wisdom with others. Perhaps we will grow more compassionate toward others.

PRACTICE: Reflecting on Reality

We can gently invite ourselves to face that which we are avoiding, thus opening ourselves to choices and goodness rather than putting down the burden of resistance and hardening ourselves. This practice of reflection can be a starting place.

Do this when you have at least twenty minutes.

Sit comfortably. Breathe naturally and allow your body to relax as much as possible. Take some time to reflect on at least one of the following realms of your life:

- Intimate relationships: partner, parents, children, siblings
- Work
- Home
- Physical health
- Religious/spiritual life

Ask yourself whether there is something you are avoiding acknowledging or are resisting. If you become aware of something, notice the resistance. What does it feel like in your body? Is there an image or a metaphor that describes it? Allow the resistance to "talk to you": What would be the worst thing that might happen if you faced the truth? What would be the best? Can you invite yourself to open a bit?

See whether there is a hope that you have about this reality. If you wish, you can express that hope as a prayer, on the order of the following:

Source of life [or whatever name for the Divine suits you] who has sustained my ancestors and me, help me to face _____. Give me strength and courage, and guide me on this path whose direction I cannot yet see. Open me to the reality before me; help me to be whole.

A BLESSING

May you face suffering with grit and grace. May you learn to see the truth of your experience. May you find the strength to understand where you are in times of darkness. And may you wrest sweetness from your pain.

8

A Time to Heal

Liberation through Forgiveness

Forgiveness is the courage to let go.
One does not pardon another;
one lets go of oneself,
thus allowing pain received and sustained,
hurt inflicted and imposed
to settle,
and the true Self to rise.

—*Rabbi Rami Shapiro*[1]

Consumed by Grievance

My friend Kathy volunteered through her synagogue as a friendly visitor with Evelyn, a synagogue member who had lived for several months in a nearby nursing home. Kathy found her weekly visits trying, as Evelyn complained bitterly about her children. They had "dumped" her in this place; they didn't invite her to live with them; they didn't care about her. Kathy tried to interest Evelyn in other topics of conversation—the synagogue, the news, Kathy's own family—but Evelyn's focus could not be pried off of her hurt and anger.

Kathy was surprised when she crossed paths with Evelyn's daughter to see her genuine concern and devotion for her mom. She learned that Evelyn's daughter visited several times a week and that she earnestly tried her best to make life as good as it could be for her mother.

Evelyn was consumed by her grievance against her family. Her anger left no energy to engage in the community in which she was living or in relationships that might have nourished her.

As we grow older, we are inevitably confronted with unfinished business from the relationships we have built over the years. Resentment and hurt can fester and even grow. This poisonous emotional baggage from the past can burden us just when we most long to be free. It can block the way toward growth and wisdom, or we can find a new way, opening to the healing power of forgiveness.

What's Wrong with Holding On to Hurt and Resentment?

All of us have amassed emotional scars by the time we pass midlife. We have probably been let down or betrayed at some point by friends, partners, co-workers, or family members. Our wounds, even if in the background, are very much alive. Carrying resentment against someone who has wounded us seems, at first glance, to be entirely justified, even righteous. I was wronged! I will never forget it! I *deserve* this anger! Many of us are nursing our grievances, perhaps even over decades, waiting for the other to take responsibility for the harm we have suffered. Sometimes the people who have injured us are no longer alive; the grievance that we carry has outlived them.

The problem is that the noxious ooze of anger and pain does not hurt the person who hurt us. Rather, it is *we* who suffer. When we hold on to our painful emotions, Rabbi Zalman Schachter-Shalomi taught, we too are imprisoned, for "the jailer spends as much time in prison as the prisoner."[2] Many elders I've known have held resentments so long that they seemed to expand, to grow so big that they have crowded out any goodness in their here-and-now lives.

Forgiving: The Promise

What if we could be liberated from the poisonous burden of resentment? What if *we* could be the agents of this release?

The Amish citizens of Nickel Mines, Pennsylvania, refused to live forever in the thrall of the unthinkable pain they endured after a deranged local man shot eleven schoolgirls, killing five of them. Almost immediately after this unimaginable crime they set about to forgive the gunman, who had turned his gun on himself and died after the attack. Townspeople from this close-knit community attended his funeral in droves, and they reached out to his mother, who in turn volunteered daily caring for one of the girls grievously injured in the attack.

One farmer in the community reflected, "Acid corrodes the container that holds it. That's what happens when we hold on to bitterness." Forgiveness for this community, according to sociologist Donald Kraybill, is not about forgetting or condoning; it is not a pardon or justice or reconciliation. Rather, it is "an act of self-preservation ... because self-pity is toxic and makes you hostage to the past."[3]

For the people of Nickel Mines, forgiveness is a decision. They do not choose to forgive because the man who destroyed innocent lives was in any way deserving of their forgiveness. Rather, those who survive forgive because holding on to rage would ruin *their* lives. Releasing ourselves from grievance softens our hearts and sweetens our lives.

A Tool from Jewish Tradition

How might we ever have the strength to make such a choice? A traditional Jewish practice invites us to exercise forgiveness on a daily basis. This prayer, which is recited at bedtime before the *Shema,* gives us practice at letting go of hurts as they happen, perhaps thereby building up the "muscle" to take on the ones we've stored up over time:

> I hereby forgive anyone who has angered or provoked me or sinned against me, physically or financially or by failing to give me due respect, or in any other matter relating to me, involuntarily or willingly, inadvertently or deliberately, whether in word or deed: let no one incur punishment because of me.[4]

This forgiveness prayer is a real-time tool for washing away hurts and resentments. It might well help us to meet tomorrow refreshed and renewed.

Perhaps you are wondering: Even if we recite these words every evening, how can words effect forgiveness? Is saying it enough? There is convincing evidence from contemporary psychology that we can change our hearts and feelings by changing our minds. The field of cognitive behavioral therapy, as expounded by Drs. Judith Beck and David Burns, has found that intervening at the level of our thoughts can alter our moods and profoundly improve our quality of life. Thus, deciding to think differently about those who have harmed us can open us to release pain and to experience more joy.

How to Forgive

Assuming we actually decide to forgive, what is the road map? Dr. Fred Luskin, director of the Stanford University Forgiveness Project, offers an accessible approach to forgiveness, which he describes as a feeling of peacefulness in the present moment. This bounty comes from deciding to free ourselves from the personal offense that has landed us in a cycle of suffering.[5] He urges us to take responsibility for our own feelings, even when we have been grievously hurt by another. He suggests that we "change the channel" on our stories of grievance by tuning in instead to people, places, and experiences that bring us beauty, gratitude, and love. We can draw from these positive emotional experiences to gain strength to forgive as we locate our own positive intentions, such as feeling more ease, being kinder, or growing as a person.

Note that forgiving requires awareness of our hurt, not denial of it. But sometimes it is difficult to even consider forgiving. We feel that forgiving the person who has harmed us means they "got away" with their crime, and we will never get justice. Forgiveness is not exoneration of the perpetrator; it is liberation for the victim. Luskin writes, "Forgiveness is the powerful assertion that bad things will not ruin your today even though they may have spoiled your past."[6]

Basically, Luskin maintains, we forgive for our own sake. How do we forgive? We do it by letting go of the quixotic expectation of recompense or justice. We do it by releasing our resentment, the poison we unwittingly turn inward upon ourselves. We forgive by training our attention on the blessings we can already count and on our deepest desire to live in a more positive way.

Forgiving is good for us, even—or especially—beyond midlife. Forgiving allows us to soften our hearts. Perhaps more concretely, forgiveness enhances our psychological, emotional, and physical health.[7] Forgiving is the pathway toward release and ease. When we release resentments and grudges, we can truly begin anew, regardless of the age at which we do so.

PRACTICE: On the Path to Forgiveness

1. Think of someone who has wronged you whom you have not forgiven. (Don't start with a really major wrong; try a minor one first!)

2. Acknowledge the pain you have felt.

3. Set an intention about what you would like to accomplish by forgiving the person who has harmed you.

4. Say the bedtime forgiveness prayer daily with this person in mind. Be sure to sit (or lie) comfortably, with your body relaxed, and to breathe deeply.

5. Pray for your well-being and healing and for that of the person who wronged you.

6. If you wish, and only if, you can let the person know that you are no longer carrying a grudge against him or her.

A BLESSING

May your heart be opened to forgiveness. May the burden of old hurts and resentments be lifted, and may you experience softening, compassion, and liberation.

9

Declaring Interdependence

Let a world of loving-kindness be built.

—Psalm 89:3 (my translation)

Julie and her husband, Jim, were traveling abroad. Julie's arthritic knees were giving her trouble, and she was finding it necessary to curtail the long, leisurely strolls that she and Jim typically shared when traveling. When they arrived at the zoo in the capital city, Julie was really worried about how she would manage. Jim suggested she use a wheelchair. Julie dubiously agreed and was delighted to find that she enjoyed every moment. When their visit was over, though, Julie warned Jim, "Don't you dare tell anyone I used a wheelchair at the zoo!"

Julie's story makes me think back to something I heard years ago in a lecture by anthropologist Jennie Keith on her research project on global aging. Keith and her colleagues had studied elders in several urban, suburban, and rural communities around the world. When they asked the question "What scares you the most about growing old?" to elders in a suburban American community, the most frequent answer was "Having to rely on others for help." Researchers observed that the older widows they studied had independently arrived at a common strategy for preparing for a trip. These older women, who lived alone in multistory homes, would first carry their empty suitcases down to the ground floor and then ferry clothing, books, and toiletries downstairs one at a time. This approach was time-consuming but worth it to them because in this way, they didn't have to ask someone else to help them carry their heavy suitcases down the stairs. It turned out that the fear of asking for or needing assistance was so great that it literally shaped these elders' actions on a daily basis.

Interestingly, elders in an African village had a very different perspective. When they were asked, "What are you most looking forward to about old age?" many of them answered, "Having someone kind to take care of me." For them, the experience of connection in being cared for was cherished, not feared. Keith writes, "In !Kung communities, interdependence is a lifelong and community-wide way of life, so that need for care is not clouded by fears that dependency will threaten personhood."[1]

How differently these two cultures approach dependency, a provocative and challenging dimension of growing older. Our North American culture views dependency as a disease, a diminution of personhood, while the !Kung culture seems to approach it as either neutral or an opportunity for expanded relationships and new roles.

Our culture exalts *independence.* The United States was forged with a Declaration of Independence. We admire people who manage by themselves. We lionize those who ask nothing of others, like the cowboy riding off into the sunset or the daughter in a TV commercial in my childhood: "Mother, please, I'd rather do it myself."

We like to imagine that we can continue to be totally independent as we get older. Deep down, though, we know that our physical or cognitive capacities are likely to wane. Sooner or later, if we live long enough, we will need someone else to help us with transportation, household tasks, financial management, or the most basic aspects of physical functioning.

In the context of such an idealization of independence, those who find themselves "counting on kindness,"[2] as social worker Wendy Lustbader puts it, feel that they have failed, that they are somehow deficient.

When I worked as a nursing home chaplain, one of my congregants was Esther, an eighty-eight-year-old widow. "Rabbi," she said, "I have helped others all my life. I helped my husband, I took care of nieces and nephews, I volunteered in my synagogue and in my organization. But now my arthritis has landed me in a wheelchair; I can't walk, I can't do anything for anyone. What good am I?"

Esther lost her sense of self-worth because she saw herself as *only* dependent. She had bought what Rabbi Abraham Joshua Heschel pointed out is a way of judging people based on what they *do* or *produce* rather than the value inherent in who they are. Rather, he suggested, "Just as the grandeur of the sun or an oak tree is not reducible to the functions it fulfills, so the grandeur of the human life is not reducible to the needs it is capable of satisfying."[3]

A teaching from the Talmud offers a very different paradigm from this rigid distinction between dependence and independence, worthlessness and value. Rabbi Yochanan, a brilliant, beautiful, and charismatic teacher, had great healing powers. He would visit a suffering fellow rabbi, take him by the hand, and "lift him up" out of his suffering. It is even said that Rabbi Yochanan could bring light into a dark room simply by rolling up his sleeves. He was literally incandescent! Yet when Rabbi Yochanan himself became ill, he relied on his colleague Rabbi Hanina to visit and heal him. The narrator of the story asks an obvious question: why does this illustrious healer need to be visited by his friend; can he not heal himself? The question is answered this way: "The prisoner cannot free himself from jail" (Talmud, *Berachot* 5b).

This text suggests that no one can survive without support from others. Even in the areas of our greatest strength or wisdom, when we ourselves face limits or difficulty we need others to lift us up.

The late Maggie Kuhn, founder of the intergenerational activist movement the Gray Panthers, rejected the dichotomy of independence and dependence. She suggested that we are always *inter* dependent. When Maggie, a lifelong social justice advocate, became crippled by arthritis and osteoporosis in her eighties, she created a new living arrangement—shared housing. She opened her home of many years to younger people, who received low-cost rent in exchange for helping with chores and personal assistance. The men and women who were blessed to share Maggie's home got far more than they gave: up-close learning from a talented, inspired leader; the satisfaction of helping her to "age in place"; and a diverse, fascinating community.

Rabbi Yochanan and Maggie Kuhn both point to the essential truth: we are all interdependent all the time. There is always some way in which we are contributing to others and some way in which we are nourished by others, even when it might appear that we are solely operating on our own or totally reliant on others.

The countercultural insight we gain from these very disparate teachers is that when we receive help from another, we also give that person an opportunity and vice versa. We can each think of many times that we have given to or helped another. No doubt, we found enjoyment and meaning in many, if not most, of these moments. On the other hand, many of us have encountered a friend or relative who was too proud to accept assistance, leaving us feeling disappointed or left out. If it is true that we are enlarged by being in relationships of caring and giving, then we might well reexamine our denial and dread of dependency.

Our loathing of dependency can cause more suffering than whatever it is that renders us in need of assistance. We may make choices that are costly for ourselves or others. The suburban widows who schlepped up and down the stairs over and over again just to avoid asking for help while packing for a trip could have risked falling and becoming even less able to remain at home. When we resist our need for help, we may become cut off from others. Worst of all, we may be filled with self-loathing as we judge ourselves and find ourselves wanting because of our need for help.

Maggie Kuhn wrote in her memoir, "In my old age I have discovered a miracle. When I reach out to others I find that I receive a new kind of energy, which is physical, mental, and spiritual. It rejuvenates and emboldens me.... [Those whom I've asked for help] have given me a confidence about asking for help, and now I don't hesitate to flag strangers down on the street and ask for help getting up a curb or into a car."[4]

We can change ourselves and our culture when it comes to interdependence. We can make conscious choices about reaching for help. We can weigh the price of avoiding dependency. We can consider the possibility of living into a vision of an interdependent, interconnected world.

We can start with ourselves, with tiny, day-to-day things. For example, when I travel by air, I like to carry my suitcase onto the plane. I have many strengths, but upper body muscle is not one of them. It is very difficult—sometimes impossible—for me to heave the suitcase into the overhead compartment. I used to clumsily try to do it myself, sometimes only to see the suitcase tumbling toward me or other unlucky souls nearby. Only then would I abashedly accept offers of help from travelers more fit than I. It occurred to me that there might be a better way. Now I am experimenting with asking another passenger to help me *before* I foolishly strain my back or put others' safety at risk. No one I've asked has ever refused. Each person has been friendly and willing. The only obstacle here has been my own judgment about dependency. I hope that practicing on the small stuff will make it easier for me to ask for—and receive—assistance when my needs are bigger and more chronic. As social worker Wendy Lustbader teaches, "Earlier in our lives, we must stop clinging to independence as if it were the only meaning of strength."[5]

Jewish spirituality pioneer Rabbi Lawrence Kushner wrote a poem that reminds us of our fundamental, blessed interconnectedness.

Jigsaw

Each lifetime is the pieces of a jigsaw puzzle.

For some there are more pieces.
For others the puzzle is more difficult to assemble.

Some seem to be born with a nearly completed puzzle.
And so it goes.
Souls go this way and that.
Trying to assemble the myriad parts.

But know this. No one has within themselves
All the pieces to their puzzle.
Like before the days when they used to seal
jigsaw puzzles in cellophane. Insuring that
All the pieces were there.

Everyone carries with them at least one and probably
Many pieces to someone else's puzzle.
Sometimes they know it.
Sometimes they don't.

And when you present your piece.
Which is worthless to you,
To another, whether you know it or not,
Whether they know it or not,
You are a messenger from the Most High.

—Lawrence Kushner[6]

PRACTICE: Asking for and Offering Help

1. Try asking someone for help once each day. Notice what feelings arise for you. Are you ashamed? Do you feel small? Now notice how the other person reacts to your request. What feelings do you detect? Do you sense judgment?

2. Pay attention to small or large opportunities to help others. Try offering help before it is solicited, as well as responding to overt requests.

3. How do you feel when you give to another? How do you view the other person?

4. Notice how you feel when someone in your life does *not* invite you to help him or her.

5. Read Lawrence Kushner's poem at least twice. Try tuning in to opportunities to bring your piece to another's puzzle.

A BLESSING

May you grow to open to ever-deeper human connection. May you find the courage to accept help, as well as to offer it. May you know that love is endless, trusting that you will only be enlarged by receiving caring as you grow older.

10

Making Wise Choices about Medical Care at the Edge of Life

> To everything there is a purpose,
> a time to everything under the heavens.
> A time to be born, and a time to die.
>
> —*Ecclesiastes 3:1–2*

As we grow older, we inevitably encounter a paradox: medical science is continually developing more marvelous capabilities to extend life, but the results of this treatment technology too often impose suffering on the person receiving it. We are caught between our love of life and of our loved ones and choices that are unprecedented and vexing. Are we obligated to do "everything" to prolong life when we or someone we love is ill? How do we know when enough is enough? When does quality of life trump the quantity of days lived?

I have learned about these medical dilemmas at the edge of life from the elders I've been privileged to accompany at the ends of their lives. Here are a few:

- Morrie, the most dapper, most life-loving ninety-six-year-old ever, suffered from an ever-spiraling decline due to congestive heart failure. On one of his many hospitalizations, his heart stopped and staff administered CPR. When he awoke some time later, Morrie said with fierce anger, "Don't ever do that to me again."
- Evelyn says, "I've had a good life for ninety-two years, but I am tired. Every night I pray that God will take me." Meanwhile, she is on oxygen, fed through a feeding tube, and awaiting surgery that her children have insisted on.
- Marjorie, a retired business owner and community activist, was seventy-eight, passionately engaged in community leadership, taking classes at a nearby university, and enjoying art, music, her husband, children, and grandchildren when she faced a recurrence of cancer. As soon as the diagnosis was confirmed, she announced to her family and friends that she had no intention of spending her final days or months in the desperate pursuit of treatments unlikely to significantly prolong her life. Instead she entered hospice care, first at home and later in-patient. She spent time with each of her many grandchildren and gave each an object from her home to remember her. She corresponded with scores of friends from various parts of her life. She died six weeks later, at peace, and an inspiration to all who knew her.

These diverse elder teachers have shown me that life is not always preferable to death, that medical treatment can sometimes be a profound burden, not a blessing. I bring their experiences and my own family's struggles in the land of illness, medicine, and choices to the consideration of medical decision making as we and our dear ones are growing older.

We who must make medical decisions at the edge of life stand on the narrow bridge between life and death. We bring to our choices the experiences we have had in caring for parents and friends, and yet each situation is unique, and the choices keep getting more complicated. We don't stand on firm ground.

To ground ourselves, we need to understand what it is about contemporary realities that make it especially difficult to make wise decisions. We need to look for guidance, which I suggest we can find from the ancient but timeless Jewish tradition. And we need tools to help us along the way.

Why Is This Decision Making So Wrenching?

Ours is an unprecedented reality. Unlike any generation before us, we have access to ever-expanding life-extending technology for ever-older people. For example, octogenarians are the most rapidly growing group of surgical patients in the United States. Heart bypass operations, stents, and angioplasty have become common for patients in their eighties and are not unusual for those in their nineties. Thirty-three percent of dialysis patients in the United States are over seventy-five. As anthropologist Sharon Kaufman notes, this almost routine utilization of high-tech and invasive medical interventions at older and older ages makes it hard to realize that there are even choices to be made—and creates enormous guilt if a patient or family member even contemplates saying *no* to treatment.

When we dread and deny death, we act as if we can stave it off endlessly by "doing something." It's easy to ignore the truth, that death may well be very near. We are sure that there must be something we can do to avoid dying. But the fact that treatment is possible and available doesn't necessarily mean it benefits the individual older person.

In my own family, I found it profoundly daunting to be part of decisions as my beloved Holocaust-survivor mother-in-law contended with countless chronic ailments and diminished memory. At eighty-six, she was nearly subjected to what would have been possibly fatal and certainly unnecessary surgery because her hospital physicians, who ran countless tests, uncovered an unusual physical condition and rushed us to decide on intervention. As it turned out, the physical condition, though real, had not been responsible for her symptoms, and what she really needed was very basic symptom management.

Dr. Dennis McCullough, a proponent of "slow medicine," writes:

> Modern medicine has complicated the situations of elders' late life by offering better and more technological means of extending the length of human life while not necessarily greatly improving its quality. Often this has meant turning what used to be a brief, acute, life-threatening illness into a kind of prolonged decline or attenuated dying.[1]

In other words, the array of possible treatments may prolong life but take away from *quality* of life.

So there *should* be decisions to be made—since use of all of this medical technology cries out for discernment. There *must* be decisions made—since most deaths in our day are deaths-by-decision. On this precipitously narrow bridge, we cannot look to medical science for the wisdom that will guide us, but we can look to Jewish tradition for anchoring values to light the way.

Guidance from Jewish Values

Five key values from Jewish tradition can guide us when we find ourselves or our loved ones on the narrow bridge between life and death. I have articulated these values in terms of decisions we might make for another, but of course they also apply to decisions we may be called to make about our own care.

The Preciousness of Life (Pikuach Nefesh)

We don't let go of life lightly. We don't dismiss the worth of even the life of the oldest old, and we certainly don't make decisions based solely on age.

There Is a Time to Die (Et Lamut)

On the one hand, life is precious and should be treasured. On the other hand, Ecclesiastes teaches, "there is a time to die" (3:2). While we are enjoined to preserve life, we are forbidden to prolong dying. Our tradition recognizes that death in its time is a blessing. When death is inevitable and imminent (the stage called *goses),* the goals of care change—no longer must we fight for every moment. Instead we must refrain from burdening the person by the things we do for them and allow them to find peace. While traditional authorities limit the application of this concept to a very narrow time frame, the value of accepting and bringing peace to death is one we can apply to a wide array of situations. This reasoning can help us accept hospice care as a valid and valuable approach when disease is advanced and further treatment is unlikely to meaningfully extend life. Hospice care can focus intervention and activity on maximizing comfort and on creating as much quality of life as is possible. Sadly, too often denial or resistance, either on the part of the family or the physician, get in the way of beginning hospice care early enough to have maximal positive impact.

Care for the Person's Physical and Emotional Needs (Kavod)

This simple value can get lost amid the swirl of high-tech treatment. We might ask: Will a proposed treatment advance the person's comfort or well-being? How well are we really caring for her? Does he have a pillow with a soft cover? Does she have her perfume? Is there music that he likes? Is whatever food she can eat really delicious?

Preserve Dignity (Mora)

One of the instructions in the Talmud for preserving an elder's dignity is "listening to his voice—not contradicting his word" (*Kiddushin* 31b). We should make decisions based on the individual's preferences, goals, and values, for ultimately only the individual can weigh the benefits or burdens of treatments. So we ask ourselves or our dear ones: What do you want now? What is most important to you? What frightens you the most? And if the person who is ill can no longer tell us, we do our very best to be an agent or a representative articulating his or her wishes, priorities, and values. It is challenging sometimes to put aside our own feelings; maybe we want to hold on to our loved one when he would dearly like to let go; maybe we feel her suffering is too hard, when she would do anything to make it to the birth of her first grandchild. Focusing on the person's perspective can clarify choices.

Healing for the Spirit (Refuat ha-Nefesh)

When we pray for healing, we pray for *refuat ha-nefesh urfuat ha-guf* ... first for healing of the soul *(refuat ha-nefesh),* then for healing of the body *(urfuat ha-guf),* then for *refuah shelemah,* or "complete healing." We learn that even when it is not possible to cure, it is always possible to bring spiritual healing, the healing that is *shalom,* "wholeness"—we can always "do something"—we can sing, touch, bless, pray, forgive, fulfill a "second-wind" dream, or just be there.

Applying Key Jewish Values

How are we to apply these timeless values to the complex choices we face on the narrow bridge we traverse as we make end-of-life choices today? We can use them as a touchstone. When faced with a decision about treatment for yourself (or for a beloved elder), you might ask:

- What is going on here?

- Am I going to "get better," or am I in the inexorable slide toward death?

When considering a proposed treatment, ask:

- Is this going to bring comfort and care?
- How else can I be cared for?
- Will having this treatment preserve my dignity?
- How can I listen to my deepest wishes and hopes?
- How can I find spiritual healing?

As anthropologist Sharon Kaufman puts it, "Are there ways, beyond the body and its medical treatment, to demonstrate worth and love?"[2]

Decision-Making Approaches

In addition to drawing on these Jewish values, a few key strategies for decision making can be helpful.

Admit That We Are All Going to Die

Facing mortality (ours and our loved ones') is the only way we can make wise and compassionate decisions about how we and they will die.

Analyze Benefits and Burdens

When considering proposed treatment and its alternatives—including the choice of no treatment—it can be very helpful to approach choices in terms of the benefits and burdens to the patient. What constitutes a burden or a benefit is completely subjective and individual, so this is measured in terms of the individual's values, preferences, and goals. What matters to you now?

Make Advance Directives

Designate a health-care proxy, someone you trust to make decisions on your behalf if you are unable to do so. Tell him or her what your wishes, values, and goals are. As you do so, it is helpful to focus on acceptable health states and valued life activities rather than particular medical interventions or technologies. Conversation, preferably multiple conversations over time, is perhaps even more critical than a written document.[3]

We will all travel the narrow bridge between life and death—as companions, with our friends and beloveds, and as our own lives reach their ends. We can hope for clarity, compassion, and companionship as we make this journey.

PRACTICE: Narrow Bridge Meditation

Situate yourself comfortably in a sitting position (or lying down, if that works better for you). Picture yourself standing on a bridge. Perhaps it is a bridge you have been on before. The one I see is a small pedestrian bridge suspended over a roaring creek in the Colorado Rockies. Notice how you feel on this bridge. Are you exhilarated by the magnificence and boundlessness of your surroundings? Are you terrified when you look down and see how far it is? Look to the other end of the bridge. Imagine yourself walking the length of the bridge, step by step. Take a few minutes to pay attention to your breath. Then ask for what you need. Perhaps you will say or think phrases like the following: may I find strength; may I find courage; may my steps be steady; may I be safe. When you have reached the far side on your visualized journey, give thanks for arriving.

A BLESSING

May you find wisdom and courage, sustenance and guidance as you walk the narrow bridge between life and death. May you and your dear ones make the journey with blessing and *shalom.*

11

New Ways of Loving

Growing Up as We and Our Parents Age

> [God] will turn the hearts of the parents toward the children and the hearts of the children toward their parents.
>
> —*Malachi 3:24 (my translation)*

My mother, who is visiting from her home two thousand miles away, is sitting at my kitchen table, sipping coffee. "So," she says, "if there is anything you want to ask me or tell me about our family, my divorce from your dad, or anything at all, I'm open." I am stunned. Is my mom, never one for emotionally laden conversation, really inviting me to ask unasked questions, to express my feelings about our shared past? It seems she is. I plunge in—mostly telling, not asking—giving voice to hurts I've carried for decades. Mom listens. She is not defensive. She does not argue. She does not apologize either. She just receives and acknowledges. Something remarkable happens. I feel better. The weight of the disappointments and resentments I'd been holding for much of my fifty-plus years has fallen away from me. I am freer, lighter.

This surprising encounter makes me wonder—what happens to relationships between parents and kids as we both age? One consequence of expanded life spans is extended years of relating to parents in midlife and beyond. While hundreds of volumes have been written about the demands and difficulties of caring for aging parents, relatively little attention has been paid to the developmental opportunities and challenges of the bond between aging parents and children outside of that dimension. Is it possible that these relationships might develop, grow, deepen, even heal over time? What would it take to consciously approach the work of "growing up" in relationship to aging parents?

Many of us are blessed with living parents even as we ourselves are growing older. It might be that long-standing rifts and conflicts will be exacerbated over time. But something else just might happen. Clinical social worker Vivian Greenberg suggests that relationships between adult children and their aging parents "can produce a balm powerful enough to heal generational wounds."[1] This "bonus" time can offer an opportunity for transformation. In this chapter, we will investigate the terrain of relationships with parents as we and they are aging, and we will explore some spiritual approaches to growing up in this domain of our lives. We will focus on the time when our parents are relatively healthy and independent. For many of us, this stage can take us into our fifties or sixties; for some of us, even into our seventies.

Confronting Vulnerability and Mortality

Watching our parents age forces us to confront vulnerability. As we see their appearance and perhaps capacities change, we realize that they are not invincible. Sooner or later we are brought to acknowledge that neither are we. It could be a relatively small thing, like seeing your mother's gray hair once she finally stops dyeing it or noticing that your dad is not hearing as well as he used to. It may be a more dramatic one, like seeing the first signs of forgetfulness in your parent. These changes are intimations not just of fragility, but also of mortality. We start to grasp, and not just in an intellectual way, that our parents will not be here forever. Since they are typically the buffer between us and mortality, we face our own mortality. One day, sooner or later, we will be "next in line."

The awareness that time is not limitless can spur us to growth in relationship with our parents. We know we do not have infinite opportunities to set things right. Maybe there is another way of being. For adult children, parents' aging is, according to Vivian Greenberg, "the last chance ... to finish their business with love, respect, and empathy."[2]

Rough Road: Carrying Our Histories with Us

My late mother-in-law, Miriam, often used to say, "Wherever I go, I take myself with me." As our parents and we age, we take both ourselves and *them* with us. We bring our histories with us into this new stage of life, including conflicts, tensions, and expectations. Often hurts or disappointments have built up over time and have led us to distance ourselves physically or psychically. As we and they face change or crisis, old, negative patterns may surface, as Vivian Greenberg suggests, "like tire tracks that have been driven on over and over again, with deeply rutted patterns and details of every tread etched in sharp relief."[3] We may very well reflexively fall into traveling on those same ingrained paths, even though we know they have not served us in the past.

Our hearts can become hardened to our mothers and fathers. Perhaps we have been scarred through confrontations or unkindness. Or maybe we've become reflexively protective and walled ourselves off. We might long for closeness and intimacy with our parents, but it has become difficult to open ourselves. Our hearts are sclerotic, covered over, inaccessible.

Circumcising Our Hearts: Becoming Available for Growth

How are we to become available for growth in relationships with parents as we all grow older? The Torah offers a wonderful image of what might be possible. In envisioning a life in covenant with God, the book of Deuteronomy promises, "The Eternal your God will open up [circumcise] your heart and the hearts of your offspring to love the Eternal your God with all your heart and soul, in order that you may live" (30:6). The image here is that the hardened matter covering our hearts will be removed so that we will have access to all of the love and tenderness within them. As we approach our most primal connections, those with our mothers and fathers, there is often a great need to break through to the heart. Growth and healing are possible, but we need to make ourselves *ready.*

> Only through truth can a person cleave to God.
>
> — *Maayan ha-Chochmah, Beshallach*

The Jewish spiritual discipline of *Mussar* offers a methodology for circumcising our hearts. Over hundreds of years, rabbis and students have endeavored to refine the soul through conscious development of key traits or virtues, called *middot.* The practice of *Mussar* involves reflecting on our actions and striving to attain holiness in relation to the *middot.* We will investigate one key trait as a focus for the effort of opening ourselves to growth in relationship to our parents: the trait of truth *(emet).*

Truth

Truth *(emet)* is the very ground on which a mature life is built. The trait of truth is concerned with our ability to see and acknowledge reality. Practicing truth means letting go of illusions and distorted thinking, meeting the world as it actually is. This is hard work, as we are prone to develop and act on our assumptions of the world around us. We don't often stop to test the veracity of those assumptions.

In the case of our parents, we might think that we "get" these people. After all, we've known them all our lives. Yet in some profound ways we humans are mysteries to one another, perhaps especially those who are closest to us. We form impressions of our parents based on our memories of them in our childhoods, but we may have glimpsed only some aspects of the whole people that our parents were, while much remained hidden from us. Moreover, even though we tend to hold on to a fixed concept of who these people are, they have likely changed over time.

Nina had a difficult relationship with her mother throughout her adult life. She had moved far away from the community where she grew up, but her hurt at her mother's criticism and distance remained with her. As her mother got older, though, Nina realized that it made sense to invite her mother to come live with her. Nina describes the two years her mother was with her as "the best time in my life." She decided, she says, to get to know her mother, on Nina's own terms. She says, "I got to see her how she saw herself, how she was in the world outside of our relationship. I saw her strengths, and I saw those qualities in myself. I got to truly love her as I never had been able to before."

> Teach yourself to say "I don't know," lest you be caught in falsehood.
>
> **—Talmud, *Berachot* 4a**

Nina met the truth of her mother's life, and it transformed their relationship. What made it possible for Nina to open herself to her mother's truth? She brought curiosity and compassion to her new encounter with her mother. This approach allowed her to appreciate her mother's life as she had not before.

When we meet our parents with curiosity, we can come to a deeper understanding of what they have undergone—the suffering, the struggles, as well as the triumphs. We can learn about how they became the way they are, especially about their lives before we came along. Looking at the truth with compassion allows us to see that our parents are flawed *human* beings. As journalist Virginia Morris puts it, we come to see each one as "both strong and vulnerable, a person who did the best he could by you and who is still doing the best he can."[4]

Facing our parents as real people helps us to grow up, to let go of grievances, and to relate as best we can in the here and now. Vivian Greenberg writes, "Children ... who see their parents as imperfect, vulnerable human beings can forgive them, discover ways to encourage intimacy with them, and live their own lives free of crippling guilt."[5] Accepting the past is not easy. One of the reasons that people hold on to anger and grievance is the deep-seated fantasy that it might yet be possible to get what they never had. When we face truth, we recognize that we cannot change whatever was difficult in the past between us and our parents. In realizing this, we may feel a profound sense of loss.

There are things to be gained by grieving those losses and moving on, however. Taking responsibility for our own lives is essential for us in order to finally grow up, for, as Vivian Greenberg warns, "if we cannot take responsibility for our own lives, despite gray hair, wrinkles, and perhaps a midlife paunch, we remain always at war with those powerful giants, our parents."[6]

If we let go of unreasonable hopes about our parents, according to Virginia Morris, we might "actually enjoy what *is* rather than constantly feeling cheated by what isn't."[7] Like Nina, we might come to appreciate our parents as we were not able to before. We can look for shared ground and savor the time we have. If it happens that our parents' difficult traits remain challenging, we will gain peace by surrendering the quest to change them. We relate to them as adults, with as much openness as we can muster. With softened hearts, we can grow more compassionate. This compassion will land not just on our parents but also on ourselves, and it can help us grow and deepen as we grow older.

PRACTICE: Cultivating Curiosity

Geriatrician Dennis McCullough suggests that adult children make a seventy-two-hour visit to their aging parent. The purpose of the visit is to take in the parent in his or her own environment, to learn about the parent's routines, connections, and sources of meaning. While it might not be practical to spend this kind of extended time with your parent, try to set aside a chunk of time to be with your parent on his or her own turf. Without assuming you know his or her life, become aware of what gives your parent pleasure, as well as what is difficult for him or her. Take time to invite your parent to tell you about his or her early life. Even if you have heard these stories before, try to bring fresh and alert attention. Ask questions to learn what your parent longed for, what brought pride, what led to disappointment.

At the end of the visit, spend some time journaling, and try to respond to some or all of these prompts.

1. What surprised me about my parent in the time we spent together was ______________________________ ____ .

2. A strength I saw in my parent was____________ ____.

3. I came to understand this about a particular flaw of my parent:_______________________________________ ____.

4. A moment I felt close to my parent was________ ____.

5. A hope I have for my parent is_____________ ____.

A BLESSING

As your parents age, may you meet them with curiosity and compassion. May you grow in understanding. May you finally find the maturity to accept them and yourself as they and you are.

12

Traveling Lighter

Winnowing "Stuff"

> The more possessions, the more worries.
>
> —*Pirke Avot 2:7*

Sheryl and Marty have lived in their gracious home in a northeastern city for over forty years. They raised their four children there, celebrated countless holidays, Shabbat meals, and birthdays, and have enjoyed myriad good times there with their beloved grandchildren. In their mid-seventies, healthy and active in their professions and the community, they decide to downsize to a condominium nearby. Sheryl and Marty love their home but look forward to letting go of some of the demands of caring for it. They are also eager to spare their children the task of combing through and disposing of decades of treasures and trash when they die.

This desired move is all about letting go. Sheryl and Marty are letting go of burdens and clutter but also of countless precious memories. They are relinquishing, at least a bit, the thread of continuity that spans these past decades. They are beginning again, traveling lighter and leaner. They will focus on what is most important: enjoying their work, their family, and each other.

Like Sheryl and Marty, you may feel pulled toward simplifying as you move beyond midlife. Perhaps, like this couple, the living arrangement that served you at an earlier phase is no longer apt for your needs and assets, whether physical or financial. Perhaps you are less interested in material comfort and more called to use resources consciously. You might even feel weighted down by accumulated papers or possessions.

It can feel daunting to downsize property. Relinquishing things that hold memories makes us feel at risk of losing our connection to the past, particularly to people and relationships that are gone. The work of sifting through piles and collections is arduous; it is easy to get lost in the sheer weight of all we have accumulated. Is it really worth it? you might wonder.

A text from *Pirke Avot,* an early Rabbinic compilation of advice for living, sheds light on the issue of acquiring and relinquishing things:

> Hillel used to say: "The more flesh, the more worms, the more possessions, the more worries, the more wives, the more sorcery, the more servants, the more misdeeds and mistrust. [On the other hand], the more Torah, the more life, the more study, the more wisdom, the more counsel, the more understanding, the more

> *tzedakah* [deeds of righteousness], the more peace."[1]

The relationship between the two halves of this teaching is intriguing. The first list involves consuming or holding things or people in utilitarian relationships. The second list features acquisitions of a life worth living. You might think that having more of the good things would be salutary, but Hillel suggests an inverse relationship between quantity and happiness. The urge to have *more* brings only unhappiness and negativity.

What do we make space for when we clear out years of piled-up papers, give up snow shoveling, or let go of that collection of dolls from around the world? According to Hillel, we open ourselves to a very different kind of pursuit. When we shift from acquiring things or people, we can attain and share wisdom and well-being.

You're not just giving up, you're *getting.* That's the message of the text—you're allowing for the possibility of enriching your life, not diminishing it. Joan Chittister suggests in *The Gift of Years* that the very urge to let go of things we have accumulated as we approach later life is a signal that we are ready to begin a new adventure: "Now, consciously or, more likely, not, we set out to find out for ourselves who we really are, what we know, what we care about, and how to be simply enough for ourselves in the world."[2]

How do we approach this work of sifting? On what basis shall we determine what is worthy of holding on to, what should be discarded? Rabbi Menachem Mendel of Satanov, also known as the Cheshbon ha-Nefesh, a great nineteenth-century teacher of *Mussar,* a Jewish spiritual discipline, offers us a lens through which we might do this discernment. Among the character traits he promotes is order *(seder),* which he defines this way: "Set all of your actions and possessions in order. Assure that every thing is in its place and time, and your thoughts are free to engage with what is before you."[3] The process that the Cheshbon ha-Nefesh suggests involves clearing out anything that distracts us from the work of the present moment. This arduous reflection and winnowing is the way we can open the door to liberation and creation in this phase of life. This is a path of discovery—of what matters now. This is a process of connecting to the past through memory, not just through keepsakes. This is a powerful way to begin again.

PRACTICE: Letting Go of Possessions

Set a goal for yourself to sift through a set of possessions in the next week. Be specific and finite: choose one drawer, corner, or pile.

Ask yourself some or all of these questions:

- Is this something that benefits me in my life right now?

• Does the time and care that this possession requires take me away from other priorities that are more important now?

• Do I feel free or weighted down when I contemplate this object?

• Is there a new configuration that would serve me better?

• If I choose to let go of this object, is there someone else who can use it?

Sort the objects into "keep," "toss," and "give away." Put the things you are keeping into an order that pleases you, and get rid of the rest, as designated.

Reflect on the process. What did you learn? What was hardest? What surprised you? There is no "right" way to do this. Try to suspend judgment and notice what you can learn about what is precious to you and what letting go means to you.

A BLESSING

May you be discerning as you relate to the things you have accumulated over your lifetime. May you release things that no longer serve you as you treasure the memories and the relationships that they represent. May this winnowing process open you to new freedom and simplicity.

13

A Sanctuary in Time

Spending Our Precious Time Mindfully

I must govern the clock, not be governed by it.

—*Golda Meir*

Reb Zalman Schachter-Shalomi, the father of the Jewish Renewal movement, faced a crisis of meaning at age sixty. Out of his depression and despair, he began preparing for old age, and he birthed Spiritual Eldering, an approach to maximizing the spiritual potential of later life. Over twenty-five years later, Reb Zalman found himself in what he called the "December" of life. He lived in Boulder, Colorado, with his wife, Eve. He spent his days in his basement study, surrounded by hundreds of leather-bound holy books, a treadmill, an easy chair, and all kinds of audio and computer equipment.

Reb Zalman was vivid and eloquent, intellectually brilliant, but physically somewhat frail. He had survived cancer; he lived with the chronic illnesses typical of a person in his ninth decade. In a series of conversations, Reb Zalman told me that he felt a tension about this time in his life. On the one hand, neuroplasticity, the brain's unending capacity to learn and grow, impelled him to do more of the teaching and creative redefinition of Judaism that had been his life's work. On the other hand, he was also feeling what he called "mitochondrial tiredness"; he recognized that his energy was more and more limited. In the couple of years before his death at nearly ninety years old, he felt drawn to confine his involvements to what was most essential.

For a number of years, Reb Zalman had been turning down most requests for lectures and interviews, and he handed over formal leadership of Jewish Renewal, the religious movement he had founded. He allowed his students to carry his work forward to the future. He said the key question we must all answer as we move toward our lives' end is "Are you saved?" He meant this not in a theological way, but rather have we made sure that we have passed on the wisdom, learning, love, and memories we wish to outlive us? At the end of his rich life, Reb Zalman focused his attention on concretizing his legacy, churning out recordings and publications of his thought, interpretations, and songs so that they would live on when he was gone, as they most certainly will do.

As we grow older, we are more and more acutely aware of the finitude of our time. We know that this present moment will not come again, and we cannot know how many more days, months, or years will be ours to live. Thus it becomes ever more urgent that we consider carefully how we are going to spend our time.

Discerning Each Day's Purpose

As we learned in chapter 1, the Slonimer Rebbe, Sholom Noach Berezovsky, taught that each day of our lives is utterly singular and irreplaceable. Every day offers a special purpose for each person; there is a cosmic repair *(tikkun)* that can only be done by *this* individual, and only on *this* very day:

> Every day has a unique purpose and role, just as does every person ... this is the meaning of "Abraham was old, come of days" [Genesis 24:1]—that Abraham came fully into every single day; he accomplished ... all of the special purposes and roles of that day.[1]

In other words, Abraham made each day meaningful.

If each of our days has a particular purpose, then it is our obligation to discern the call of this day or of this time in our lives. To achieve each day's or period's purpose, we must be aware of what draws us—and to clear space to make it possible for us to respond. This is what Reb Zalman demonstrated by turning down invitations and tasks that were no doubt appealing but not aligned with his core priority and diminished energy.

It could be that activities or roles that are on our "docket" were once important to us but no longer bring us satisfaction. We may be continuing to do them to please others or because it is difficult to admit to ourselves that we no longer wish to participate in them. It could also be that we have yearnings to which we have not yet responded—aspirations to learn, to experience, or to contribute in ways we have never done before. Or perhaps we are feeling a pull to settle in, grow quiet, to spend time simply *being,* not just *doing.*

How are we to manage this discernment? Personally, I struggle with this constantly. I find myself becoming overly busy, my calendar packed with engagements that are all individually compelling but when put together make for more harried, stressed days than I would like. So, I prune—I examine my commitments, cut out some to leave a more spacious schedule. I always feel relieved and never, ever regret having dropped an activity from my portfolio. I swear that I will not become overprogrammed again. But then, like the jungle that ineluctably overgrows the house in Gabriel Garcia Márquez's *One Hundred Years of Solitude,* new commitments crop up, I say "yes" more than "no," and once again I am too, too busy. I, like so many of us, suffer from what geriatrician Dr. Bill Thomas calls in his book *Second Wind* "time poverty and hurry sickness."[2]

My struggle with too many time commitments is one kind of dilemma around mindful use of time. Another common struggle is the sense that time is too empty, what the author Florida Scott-Maxwell called in her memoir on aging, *The Measure of My Days,* "a desert of time."[3] Some of us find it difficult to think of what it is that we want to be doing. Or we have physical limitations that get in the way of our desires. My sister, Jill, seriously ill with cancer, found herself having to make hard choices, stewarding her limited strength in order to do what was most valuable to her or those she loved.

What's Most Important?

We need to be mindful of what is central to us at all times so that we will choose activities and projects that are harmonious with this moment's core call. You might ask yourself:

- What is *this* time of my life for?
- What is it *not* for?

Perhaps this time of life is an opportunity for discovering new ways to inhabit time. If we have been busy, busy, busy all the time, we might experiment with designating time to simply *be.* We could sit in meditation, enjoy nature, or listen to music. If we have been task oriented and serious minded, perhaps we will explore ways to play or to find pleasure, whether through new engagements or through giving ourselves permission to spend time in ways we have always loved but for which we never made the time.

We might find new ways of using our skills to help others. If we have been focused on caring for others, we might take time to discover how we can use time to care for ourselves.

The Shomer Strategy: Getting Help to Fully Inhabit Our Days

Perhaps we need, as a friend of mine suggested, a *shomer* (keeper), a friend or colleague who will remind us of the call we have committed to answering, perhaps gently challenging us if we have become distracted or too busy to attend or if we seem to be having difficulty mobilizing ourselves. We could arrange for regular check-ins with our *shomer.* In this way, we can help one another to stay aligned, to fully inhabit our days.

And certainly we need to remain flexible, for one day's task is not another's. What may have drawn us last year or last month may not be the thing for today or tomorrow. This task of mindfully spending time requires attention, honesty, and openness. This is sacred work, for time is a key dimension in which we humans experience the holy, as Rabbi Abraham Joshua Heschel taught in a brilliant address to the 1961 White House Conference on Aging: "Time is perpetual presence, perpetual novelty. Every moment is a new arrival, a new bestowal. Just to be is a blessing, just to live is holy. The moment is the marvel."[4]

PRACTICE: Setting Your Intention

1. Take a chunk of time (a week, for example) as an experiment.

2. Sit quietly and reflect on what is most important for you to accomplish in this period. Form an intention *(kavvanah)* for this period. What is the most important task or sensibility for you now?

3. Look at your calendar and reflect on your commitments in light of this. Is there anything that you have scheduled that would get in the way of your *kavvanah?* Is there anything that you want to "slot into" your calendar? Anything you want to remove?

4. After the time period has passed, reflect on how well you stuck to your *kavvanah.* What would you do differently? What distracted you from your intention? You may want to journal as a way of harvesting what you've learned.

A BLESSING

May you fulfill the promise of your minutes, hours, and days. May you grow in patience. May you stretch to discover new ways to spend and treasure time, as the Psalmist teaches, "Teach us to count our days rightly, that we may obtain a wise heart" (Psalm 90:12).

Part III

Basking in the Light

Honing and Sharing Wisdom

14

Answering the Call

Saying "Here I Am" *(Hineini)*

> Reaching old age means summoning up the inner resources that enable a person to rise and accomplish his purpose in life.
>
> *—Rabbi Menachem Mendel Schneerson, the Lubavitcher Rebbe*

A movie theme song memorably asked, "What are you doing the rest of your life?" This can be a burning question for us as we grow older. Whether we manage to formally retire from work or simply itch for new focus, the question of our life's purpose and meaning can be acute beyond midlife. For many of us, changes in work or family will open up the possibility of new pursuits, whether vocational or avocational. On the other hand, the absence of previous roles and engagements may leave us feeling confused about our identity or life's purpose. We have only to look at TV commercials for retirement planning featuring vibrant older people skydiving, golfing, or walking on the beach to realize that our secular culture urges us to focus on recreation and subtly suggests that we no longer have to worry about making a difference in the world. The problem with this model is that, untempered, it leads to emptiness and desolation. As the brilliant theologian Abraham Joshua Heschel taught, overemphasis on recreation leads to "the trivialization of existence."[1]

Interestingly, the central heroes of the Torah, Abraham and Moses, received their callings beyond midlife. Abraham was seventy-five when he was commanded to leave behind his birthplace, extended family, and all that was familiar to set off for "the land that I will show you" (Genesis 12:1). Moses was an eighty-year-old shepherd working for his father-in-law when he happened upon the strange and amazing sight of a burning bush and was tapped to lead his people out of slavery toward the Promised Land. Each of them responded to the divine call with this word: *hineini*—"here I am." Each of them dropped everything and turned toward challenge. Why did the Divine not choose young, fresh heroes and leaders? Perhaps because of the experience and accrued perspective that these men were able to bring to their tasks. As they said *hineini,* they drew on their earlier life experience and declared themselves ready to embark in remarkable ways onto paths of wonder and significance as they were growing older.

We will likely not have callings quite as outsized as those of Abraham and Moses in what sociologist and storyteller Sara Lawrence-Lightfoot calls our "third chapter"—after childhood and adulthood—and what cultural anthropologist Mary Catherine Bateson calls "second adulthood." But we can, if we open ourselves, surely become aware of the pull to give, learn, contribute, serve, or create. In this chapter, we will explore an approach to calling grounded in Jewish tradition. We will examine the callings available to us beyond midlife—how we can recognize them and how we might find our way as we respond to them. In doing so, we can realize what Lawrence-Lightfoot describes in her book *The Third Chapter:* "We [need not] assume a trajectory of decline after fifty but recognize this as a time of potential change, growth, and new learning, a time when 'our courage gives us hope.'"[2]

The Mitzvah Model

We can understand the notion of callings in a Jewish context through the concept of mitzvot. Mitzvot are traditionally understood as divine commandments, but for our purposes, we might see them as invitations to holiness or opportunities to widen our horizons and deepen our connections. The mitzvah model offers us a possibility for meaning and significance as long as we live.

In a traditional Jewish understanding, the individual is bound to God through the covenant forged at Mount Sinai. God promised to accompany the Jewish people through all time, and the Jewish people committed, in return, to be faithful in relationship with the Divine. The behavioral manifestation of that pact are mitzvot—the ritual and ethical laws contained in the Torah and explicated by the sages through the generations. In the postmodern era, it may be that you do not accept the enumeration of commandments as outlined by the Rabbis or contemporary religious authorities. Instead, you may live out the covenant by learning about and attending to the demands of tradition and then discerning your own sense of what you are called to do in the domains of obligations in the interpersonal realm, such as ethics, and in the realm of human-divine interrelationship, such as ritual and spiritual practice.

In an insight that is as profoundly countercultural today as it was when he articulated it in an address to the 1961 White House Conference on Aging, Rabbi Abraham Joshua Heschel suggested that it is through the experience of being obligated that one truly exists. The notion that we continue to be obligated means we are engaging in the central human task of repairing and redeeming the world *(tikkun olam)* through observance of the mitzvot. According to Rabbi Heschel:

> What a person lives by is not only a sense of belonging but a sense of indebtedness. The need to be needed corresponds to a fact: something is asked of a man, of every man. Advancing in years must not be taken to mean a process of suspending the requirements and commitments under which a person lives. To be is to obey. A person must never cease to be.[3]

The state of obligation to mitzvot offers a "sense of significant being." This potential for meaning has no end point. There is no retirement from a life of mitzvot nor any senior citizen discount. We are called to hallow our lives every day for as long as we live. In this understanding, as we grow older, we are as bound to mitzvot as any other adult. We sense that something is expected of us, that our actions matter, that we can transcend recreation and emptiness. This is a refreshingly different message from the ones transmitted by our contemporary culture.

We are always connected, always called, to hear and respond to the call of the mitzvah. What happens, though, if our capacity is limited by illness, disability, or frailty? This duty to mitzvah is a sliding-scale obligation. We are called to perform the mitzvah as fully as we can. So, for example, if we were to feel called to engage in daily prayer, the center of the three daily liturgies we'd be praying would be a set of blessings called the *Amidah. Amidah* means "standing," as these prayers are traditionally said while standing. What if you cannot stand? Then, according to the Rabbis, you sit. What if you don't have the stamina to recite all nineteen blessing? Then you say an abridged summary of them. What if you cannot speak? You meditate on the prayers. In each of these cases, you are considered to have fully discharged your obligation. The same would be true of the obligation to engage in deeds of caring, *gemilut chasadim.* If you cannot prepare a meal or make a visit to a person in your community who is ill, perhaps you can make a phone call or send a note. You have responded to the call, you have engaged in holiness. The call is always within your ken, as God tells the Israelites:

> Surely, this mitzvah which I enjoin upon you this day is not too baffling for you, nor is it beyond reach. It is not in the heavens, that you should say, "Who among us can go up to the heavens and get it for us and impart it to us, that we may observe it?" Neither is it beyond the sea, that you should say, "Who among us can cross to the other side of the sea and get it for us and impart it to us, that we may observe it?" No, the thing is very close to you, in your mouth and in your heart, to observe it. (Deuteronomy 30:11–14)

The message of the mitzvah model, then, is that later life is a time when much is asked of us and when we have much to give. The mitzvah model suggests to those of us who are growing older that our actions matter, that we have the means to transcend the narrow confines of our lives' current context. The key questions for us beyond midlife are thus: What is the mitzvah I'm called to perform at this moment in my life? What can I contribute out of or even in spite of my difficulties?

What Mitzvah Calls You?

We come full, not empty, to the callings beyond midlife. Mary Catherine Bateson says that we bring with us wisdom garnered from experience, combined with energy, and at least some freedom. She calls this rich accumulation "active wisdom."[4] But how do we determine which mitzvah calls us now? There are so many possibilities.

Many people at the cusp of big change, such as retirement, feel overwhelmed by the vast choices before them. Should they take a course? A trip? Get a job? What will they say when someone asks, "What are you doing these days?" It is challenging to figure out what is most compelling when we don't have an external structure to guide us. To what do we want to say *hineini*—"here I am"?

One way of categorizing the mitzvot comes from this teaching from *Pirke Avot:* "The world stands on three things: on *Torah* [learning], on *avodah* [spiritual practice], and on *gemilut chasadim* [caring connection]" (1:2). You might consider these categories when exploring what mitzvah draws you now:

> *Torah:* Do you want to learn something new or return to a subject or skill you once enjoyed? Are you intrigued by teaching something in which you've gained some expertise?

> *Avodah:* Do you want to go inside, to grow more aware of yourself through personal growth? Do you want to try on practices to find greater spiritual connection, such as prayer, meditation, or yoga? Do you want to engage your creative side in art, music, writing, or crafts?

> *Gemilut chasadim:* Do you want to mentor or nurture others? Do you wish to reach out to care for family members, neighbors, or strangers? Might you want to advocate for those who are bruised by social injustice?

Look Back to Give Forward

One way to identify the callings that pull you is to examine your past—as Sara Lawrence-Lightfoot puts it, "Looking back and giving forward."[5] Look for pursuits and engagements that gave you pleasure or meaning earlier in your life. You might notice threads you dropped, as did Aliza, one of my students in an independent living residence, who had always been interested in art and finally had a chance to seriously study painting around the time she retired. Even if you are doing something that is entirely new to you, you will, like Abraham and Moses, bring all that you have done and learned to this calling.

You might notice parts of yourself that you did not have a chance to engage, as did eleven of my students in their eighties and nineties who decided to study for and celebrate their belated bat mitzvah together. Perhaps you were an activist in your youth but put that aside in the face of the demands of career or family, and now you will be drawn again to the work of repairing the world. This work might become a job, what social innovator and author Marc Freedman calls "encore careers," which he says represent "a kind of practical idealism at the intersection of continued income, deeper meaning, and social impact."[6] Or perhaps it is a nonpaying passion, such as that shared by a group in Philadelphia called the Granny Peace Brigade. Here is a description of them from the *Philadelphia Inquirer:*

> The Granny Peace Brigade gathered at noon in Rittenhouse Square, nine of them. They divided up their 400 leaflets and took their positions. Evelyn Alloy, 96, pushed her walker across 18th Street, in front of TD Bank, and covered the corner like a middle linebacker. Nobody got by her. "We're for peace, not war," she said. People had to work hard not to take her flier. She shoved it at them, pushed it, as much as any feathery, frail woman one week shy of 97 could push or shove.
>
> "Don't join the Army. Stay at home, sir," she said to a man walking by in a FedEx uniform. "Oh, I will," he replied kindly, taking her flier.

> A man holding hands with a woman walked by in a T-shirt that said, "Where is the Finish Line [a sporting goods store]?" "The finish line is the end of war," Alloy said.[7]

Experiment

The terrain beyond midlife is new to us and, in a sense, new to the world. It is unprecedented to have decades of life to engage beyond childbearing and career. We don't have many models—this is not your grandfather's or grandmother's aging. So we need to be adventurers and explorers. As explorers, we should be prepared for false starts, for paths that lead to no particular destination. We may respond to a call, try a mitzvah, and find ourselves unsatisfied, uncomfortable, or under-stimulated. So we try another.

After partially retiring, Jonathan decided to go back to school for an advanced course of study in his field. He found that the very intellectualized discourse did not draw him. He realized that what most attracted him was a particular side of the work he had already been doing. After self-reflection, with the help of a spiritual director, he happily dropped school and reinvested in his work.

We need to give a mitzvah time, reflect, adjust, and be ready to let go of this one if it doesn't feel right. This is part of the journey. It is not a failure to try on something that doesn't grab us; it is an act of bravery to admit it. We may start over again and again as we seek purpose later in life. This is not only because not every calling turns out to be compelling but also because we keep changing and readying ourselves for new callings.

We may need a period explicitly dedicated to exploration without firm commitments in order to discern our callings. Marc Freedman proposes a "grown-up gap year" for this purpose.[8] Of course, most of us don't have the wherewithal to withdraw from work or other commitments completely, but we may find it fruitful to dedicate some of our free time for this experimentation.

Even a calling we take on and stick with may change as our capacities change. It could be that we will need to wrestle with the question of how much is enough, as does Peg, who is seventy-four. She has accomplished a great deal in an illustrious career, offers her skills in community organizations, and still wonders how she could ever feel complete with what she has done to help this troubled world. She is comforted, she says, by the teaching from *Pirke Avot* 2:21: "It is not your obligation to complete the task, but neither are you free to desist from it."

But what if you can't do what you used to or what you aspire to? We learn from the mitzvah model that our calling is to fulfill the mitzvah to the best of our abilities. We need to be honest with ourselves about what we are able to do and what is too much. This requires humility; it is so easy to get our pride wrapped up in what we are able to do and how.

A way of thinking about this is an instruction I heard once from a yoga teacher. The task, she said, is to do a pose until it is full—effortful, perhaps challenging, but not painful or injurious. That, she said, *is* the practice—living in that tension between stretching to capacity and accepting limits. It is not about how perfectly we can stretch to do a particular pose but that we have stretched as far as we can safely go.

Our mitzvah, our calling, can be full, whether we are working at it eight hours a day or having a few minutes of engagement with it. It can be full if we are doing it from a desk or a wheelchair, if we get to the task by car, book, or computer. Maggie Kuhn, the late founder of the Gray Panthers advocacy group, was a lifelong activist and rabble-rouser. When she had reached her eighties and was living with crippling arthritis, she wrote in her memoir *No Stone Unturned:*

> What can we do, those of us who have survived to this advanced age? We can think and speak. We can remember. We can give advice and make judgments. We can dial the phone, write letters, and read. We may not be able to butter our bread, but we can still change the world.[9]

PRACTICE: What Mitzvah Calls You Now?

Settle yourself into a comfortable place. Have with you a journal or other place to write (computer is fine, if this is best for you). Allow yourself to be comfortable, not pressed for time.

Take some time to think about callings in your life. You might want to reflect on the categories of mitzvot we explored in this chapter:

- *Torah:* learning and teaching
- *Avodah:* spiritual practice, prayer, creativity
- *Gemilut chasadim:* caring connection to others, to the world

Take on a mitzvah from one of these categories (or not, if something else draws you) for the next month. Reflect on how it calls to you, what is challenging in responding *hineini*—"here I am." At the end of the month, reflect on the experience of responding to the call of this mitzvah. What was satisfying? What was provocative? What was difficult? Decide at the end of the month whether you will continue with this mitzvah and/or take on a new one.

A BLESSING

May your heart open to that which calls you at this time in your life. May you be adventurous and bold in responding to new challenges. May you stretch yourself and accept your limitations. May you add beauty and goodness to the world through your mitzvot.

15

Drawing from the Well

Developing a Blessing Practice

> There are only two ways to live your life. One is as though nothing is a miracle. The other is as though everything is a miracle.
>
> —*Albert Einstein*

Cherie has been coping for the past couple of years with a seriously ill family member and a child with disabilities. She manages not just to put one foot in front of the other but to remain vibrantly engaged in her work and to give her kids enough of whatever they need. No matter how exhausted she feels, she seems to be able to draw strength to stay present to her children. When I ask her how she finds resiliency in this time of immense difficulty, she says, "The only way to get through this is to have an inner life." For Cherie, having an inner life includes spiritual practices such as meditation and yoga, which offer her solace and grounding.

Cherie's capacity to access life-giving resources reminds me of the biblical account of the matriarch Rebecca. Eliezer sets off on a journey to find a worthy mate for Isaac, son of his master, Abraham. Eliezer identifies Rebecca as the perfect candidate. The qualities that demonstrate her aptness are her kindness and generosity. Eliezer meets Rebecca at a well, where she is drawing sustenance for herself and for her father's flocks. Unbidden, Rebecca offers this stranger water and returns again and again to the well until he and all of his animals have received the sustenance they need (Genesis 24).

Rabbi Yael Levy teaches that Rebecca models the capacity to draw strength in order to nurture both ourselves and others. Rebecca returns to the well again and again, drawing endless buckets of water so that everyone's needs are met. Rabbi Levy teaches that spiritual practice can be a wellspring of nourishment and succor for us, one to which we can return again and again in crisis and in ordinary time.[1]

In the complex experience of growing older, we can draw on spiritual practice as a wellspring of resiliency. Developing regular practices can support us as we encounter pain. Practice can serve as an anchor to ground us as so much changes in and around us. Practice can bolster us when we feel isolated and comfort us amid loss. In all of these challenging experiences, when we might feel the urge to deaden ourselves, to withdraw or disconnect, practice can help us stay present and connected.

The Wellspring of Blessings

In Jewish tradition, the practice of blessings offers a way to elevate the mundane, to draw our attention to the present moment, and to connect us to ourselves and to others. Here we will focus on three specific spiritual practices related to blessings:

- *Saying* blessings to mark and give thanks for the experiences we have, such as eating, awakening, encountering people, and being in nature
- *Sending* blessings in meditation to develop heightened compassion for ourselves and for others
- *Offering* blessings to others to invoke goodness and deepen connection

But first, we need to acknowledge that there are obstacles to engaging in life-giving spiritual practices such as these.

The Stone Occludes the Well: Obstacles to Spiritual Practice

The well of spirituality can nurture and nourish us, but many of us find it hard to bring ourselves to it.

The patriarch Jacob found himself by a well in a field on his journey as he fled his brother. Like his mother, Rebecca, he sought sustenance from the well. He was thirsty, and so were the flocks of the local shepherds, who had apparently been unable to budge a heavy stone that was covering the well. Jacob managed to move the stone, and thus the flocks were watered and he was revived (Genesis 29).

Like Jacob, we often find ourselves blocked from accessing that which can sustain us. We might suspect that spiritual practices would be grounding or inspiring, yet we encounter hurdles in taking them on. We are so busy. Our contemporary culture prizes productivity. Even if we are not working or not doing so full-time, we fill our time with activities and obligations. It feels difficult to carve out time for spiritual practice, which doesn't necessarily yield tangible outcomes or products.

We are not just busy; we are also distracted. Our attention is drawn in many directions at once. It is challenging to put aside our mobile phones and computers, to step away from the incessant stream of news, social networking, emails, and external demands. Because technology makes stimulation and communication available 24/7, it is easy to lose any hint of downtime.

Busyness and distraction are powerful barriers to engaging in life-giving spiritual practice. But there is a barrier that is even more profound. Spiritual practice puts us in touch with our feelings, which can be frightening, maybe even terrifying. We often resist noticing or acknowledging our deepest fears, our sadness, and our feelings of inadequacy. Researcher Brene Brown observes in her book *Daring Greatly* that we are terrified by vulnerability, which she defines as uncertainty, risk, and emotional exposure. Paradoxically, she notes, it is precisely by recognizing and sharing vulnerability that we can forge connection to others and live most fully. It is our shame at not being perfect or good enough that prevents us from living in our vulnerability.[2] Through spiritual practice, such as blessings, we can touch and *use* our vulnerability to make greater wholeness.

I want to note one final obstacle to spiritual practice—the erroneous belief that we do not know enough to be able to do the practices. This is an issue for many people, including many Jewish people, who fear that their lack of familiarity with Hebrew or facility with traditional rituals makes them incompetent at spiritual practice. It can be intimidating, to be sure. But I want to assure you that there is always a place to start. For Jews, the tradition is your inheritance; it is a treasure chest that came with you when you were born or converted, and you can open it at any time. You can investigate everything in the chest or just take out a single shiny object (custom). It is yours; do not let yourself be intimidated or discouraged.

Three Approaches to Blessing Practice

If you feel the urge to find a means of accessing more connection, more truth, more sustenance, then these three blessing practices can be vessels for drawing forth goodness.

Saying Blessings: Honing Gratitude

Saying blessings of gratitude can be a fruitful place to begin exploring your spiritual practice. Gratitude is the opposite of taking life for granted. Intensifying our sense of gratitude draws us more and more into the here and now. Psychologist Dr. Sonja Lyubomirsky writes in *The How of Happiness,* "The practice of gratitude involves a focus on the present moment, on appreciating your life as it is today and what has made it so."[3] Gratitude draws our attention to what is good, right, and dear. It guides us away from boredom, dissatisfaction, and despair.

Gratitude is a focus of nearly every great spiritual tradition, and it has recently caught the attention of the field of positive psychology. Researchers have discovered that gratitude can enhance our physical, emotional, and interpersonal well-being. For example, researcher Robert Emmons reports in his book *Thanks,* "People who regularly keep a gratitude journal report fewer illness symptoms, feel better about their lives as a whole, and are more optimistic about the future."[4]

> We give thanks to You ... for Your miracles that are with us each day; and for Your wonders and favors in every season—evening, morning, and afternoon.
>
> **—*Amidah* prayers, daily prayer book**

Yehudim, the Hebrew word for "Jews," means "thankful ones." Not surprisingly, gratitude is a central virtue in Jewish tradition. Gratitude is cultivated through the practice of saying blessings throughout the day's activities and experiences. In the Talmud, we are taught that a person must recite one hundred blessings a day (*Menachot* 43b). The blessings this passage is discussing are liturgical bene-dictions. In Jewish tradition you offer a benediction, a *berachah,* to acknowledge the wonders of nature, like seeing the sea or a beautiful tree or hearing thunder. You say a *berachah* before performing a commanded act, like lighting Shabbat candles, and you recite a benediction when you experience sensory enjoyment or satisfaction, like when you eat, drink, or go to the bathroom. You say a *berachah* when you hear good news, when you see a wise person, and even when someone dies. It's easy to see how you can get to one hundred in a day!

Here are a few examples:

On seeing fruit trees in the spring:

- Blessed are You, Eternal our God, Sovereign of all time, for this world, which lacks nothing, for lovely creatures and beautiful trees, for the pleasure we humans experience.

On hearing thunder:

- We bless You, Eternal our God, Sovereign of all time, Your might and power fill the world.

  On seeing lightning, shooting stars, mountains, or the sunrise:

- Blessed are You, Eternal our God, Sovereign of all time, for the work of creation.

  On hearing good news:

- We bless You, Eternal our God, Sovereign of all time, You are good and You bring goodness.

  On hearing bad news:

- We bless You, Eternal our God, Sovereign of all time, Your justice is true.

  On going to the bathroom:

- Blessed are You, Source of creation, You created human beings with wisdom, filling us with openings and vessels. It is obvious to You that if one were to open or close inappropriately, it would be impossible for us to stand before You. Blessed are You, wondrous Healer of all flesh.

We often are so caught up in the stuff of our lives that we don't actually notice what we are doing or experiencing. Rabbi Yossi, a sage cited in the Talmud, teaches, "Alas for people who see but don't know what they see and for people who stand but don't know on what they stand" (Talmud, *Chagigah* 12b). Pausing to offer a blessing draws our attention to the fact that we are eating, or seeing a flowering tree, or performing a ritual. We become more aware, more present, more grateful. Even mundane experience becomes infused with holiness. Reciting blessings directs our attention to goodness, even in the midst of challenge or struggle. This is an ancient and potent practice of mindfulness.

PRACTICE: Saying Blessings throughout Your Day

• See how many times a day you can pause to utter a blessing. You could find versions of blessings in any daily prayer book, or you can simply make your own. When you are having a sensory experience or doing a mitzvah, pause a moment, take a breath, and give thanks/praise.

• Try any of these openers to create your own blessings—or make up your own.

• *Baruch atah Adonai...*

• We bless You, Eternal our God...

• Blessed is the Eternal, Source of the universe...

• Blessed are You, Eternal, Sovereign of the universe...

• Try to enjoy the practice—don't feel that it's a contest and that the more blessings, the better. You may find it easier to start with a couple of blessings a day, so that you can savor the experience you are having, as well as the experience of blessing.

Rebbe Nachman of Breslov taught that our souls long to feel grateful: "Gratitude rejoices with her sister, joy, and is always ready to light a candle and have a party."[5]

Sending Blessings: Honing Compassion

In Jewish tradition, one vision of perfection is in this phrase from the Psalms: "Let a world of loving-kindness [*chesed]* be built" (89:3, my translation). The attribute of loving-kindness is understood as boundless, overflowing love unfettered by conditions or restraints. The verse teaches that our aim in this world—and maybe even beyond—is to grow love and compassion. The project of expanding our hearts, making more room for kindness, is a central Jewish enterprise. The fruit of our endeavors can be another understanding of this phrase: the word *olam,* which can mean "world," can also mean "eternity." If we grow in our capacity to feel and share love, then, we can hope, forever will loving-kindness be established.

Sending blessings to ourselves and to others can deepen the wellspring of compassion within us. There is amazing power to wishing well for a person, even yourself. And wishing another well, even someone whom you find difficult, can soften the heart and awaken understanding. If we do this even when we don't feel like it, we will find that we have more compassion to bring to everything in our lives. The Rabbis teach that when we perform a mitzvah without particular intention, we cultivate intention, and almost despite ourselves, we soon find that the act that began mechanically is now coming straight from the heart.

Toward this aim of deepening loving-kindness, we can draw from *metta,* a Buddhist structure for sending blessings of compassion.[6] *Metta* means "loving-kindness," a close parallel to *chesed.* In *metta* meditation, we sit quietly, breathing comfortably, and follow a sequence of extending loving-kindness—first toward ourselves. It might seem strange to send blessings to yourself. Most likely if you were to tune in to your inner dialogue, you would find that you quite often speak to yourself in a way that is far from loving: Why did you say that? Buck up, why are you sitting around complaining? Why can't you be like...? If you give blessing yourself a try, you may find that it is surprisingly moving.

After ourselves, we extend blessing to what the Buddhists call a patron, a person who is good to us, about whom we have unambiguously positive feelings. This could be a teacher, a mentor, a friend, or a neighbor.

Next we send blessings to a neutral person. This is someone toward whom we have neither strong positive nor negative feelings. The neutral person could be someone you interact with in your daily round but with whom you don't have a deep relationship. I have often chosen a person who works at my neighborhood food store as my neutral person. It has been quite delightful to meet up with this person after I have sent her blessings. I feel very warmly toward her, connected to her in an unspoken way.

We follow the neutral person with a dear one (friend, partner, sibling). We send blessings to this person, channeling concern, worry, and love into heartfelt wishes for his or her well-being. Finally, having warmed up the loving-kindness in our hearts, we extend blessing toward a person with whom we have some kind of conflict or ambivalent feelings. Initially, it is good to select someone with whom we have a problem but not the most hurtful person in our lives (that might come later). Choose a neighbor who has annoyed you, a relative by whom you felt slighted, a friend by whom you felt disappointed. Don't worry about whether this blessing is entirely sincere. Just try your best to wish for this person's well-being. Doing this regularly may help you feel more kindly toward this person. Out of this warm sensibility may emerge greater understanding and even forgiveness. I have found this to be enormously helpful when riding in the car with a surly adolescent child, by the way!

PRACTICE: Try Sending Blessings

It is customary in loving-kindness meditation to use three or four phrases in sending blessing. I have reached into Jewish tradition to develop blessing phrases. Each one of these phrases comes from a prayer in the traditional siddur (prayer book).

Here are phrases you can say in sending blessing to yourself, to a benevolent person, to a neutral person, to a dear one, and to a difficult person:

For Yourself

May I feel safe.	*Shemor et nafshi.*
May I feel satisfied.	*Sabeini mituvecha.*
May I be healed.	*Refa'eini va'arapeh.*
May I find peace.	*Sim li shalom.*

For Another Person ("f" for a woman; "m" for a man)

May you feel safe.	*Yishmor et nafshech.* (f)
	Yishmor et nafshecha. (m)
May you feel satisfied.	*Yasbiech metuvo.* (f)
	Yasbiecha metuvo. (m)
May you be healed.	*Yirapech vateirapi.* (f)
	Yirapecha vateirapeh. (m)
May you find peace.	*Yasim lach shalom.* (f)
	Yasim lecha shalom. (m)

When you have practiced sending blessings in this way, you may wish to extend your blessings even further; send these blessings to your neighborhood, to your community, to your country, to the entire world. May the world be filled with ever more loving-kindness.

Offering Blessings: Fostering Connection

When I worked as a chaplain in an eldercare community, I noticed over time that my congregants almost always offered me beautiful wishes as we parted after a visit. I came to treasure these spontaneous blessings, which were varied and abundant:

> God should let you live to be my age, and well.
>
> I wish you everything you wish yourself.
>
> May God grant you the happiness I've known.
>
> May we live and be well and be here together next year.
>
> May God bless you with a future that is unprecedented, and may your congregants appreciate the meaning of your message.

Some elders used the language of faith, others simply offered loving, sincere hopes. However they were articulated, these blessings were powerful. They made our encounters explicitly reciprocal; we were each giving to the other in a holy way. Moreover these blessings connected the two of us to the Transcendent, the Source of life and love. Finally, blessings connected both of us to hope for the future. These elders fulfilled a precious dimension of aging, the capacity to be a source of blessings. They live forever in my heart through their blessings, which resonate still, many years later.

Offering blessings is a natural element of human relating, but perhaps one with which many of us have lost touch. The blessings I've received from people I've served have inspired me to integrate blessings into my everyday interactions. I encourage you to try this as well.

PRACTICE: Try Offering Blessings to Others

I invite you to try offering blessings. You may already do this in the form of sending cards or notes. In our detached, digital age, a handwritten note expressing wishes for speedy recovery, condolences, or just warm greetings is a precious communication. Perhaps thinking of those interactions as blessings will shift in some way how you go about them or simply help you value them all the more.

You can offer blessings in person in the context of conversations with friends, neighbors, or family members. You can do it when someone you care about is in distress or overflowing with joy. You can bless as a part of saying good-bye.

Here are a few suggestions for words you might use to offer blessings:

- May you...
- I wish you...
- I hope that...
- May God bless you with...

Be creative; don't worry about the words, but focus on your hopes for the person you are blessing or on his or her hopes for him- or herself. You may feel shy at first about giving blessings. It's always fine to ask permission. It's also great to start with someone you feel very comfortable with. A blessing habit is a beautiful thing. When you offer blessings, you become a conduit for connection—to hopes, to Power in the universe you hope will act/respond on behalf of the other, to eternity, and to the heart of the person before you.

A BLESSING FOR BLESSING

These three blessing practices—saying blessings, sending blessings, and offering blessings—enable us to touch something bigger than ourselves. In *Blessing: The Art and the Practice,* theologian David Spangler writes that blessings remind us that "we are made of spirit stuff, soul stuff, love stuff ... and therefore kin to life and to each other."[7]

May these blessing practices enrich and deepen your everyday experience, and may you be able to draw on this wellspring in moments of challenge, suffering, and joy.

Afterword

> An elder ... is a person whose work is to synthesize wisdom from long life experience and formulate this into a legacy for future generations.
>
> *—Barry and Debby Barkan and the elders of the Live Oak Institute*

The journey beyond midlife is not only a matter of surviving or even flourishing for ourselves. Ultimately, we are called to plant seeds for the benefit of those who come after us. This message is powerfully depicted in a Talmudic legend about Rabbi Honi the Circle Maker:

> Honi was walking on a road one day when he saw an old man planting a carob tree. Honi was taken aback by the sight of this person advanced in years laboring to plant a tree. "How old are you?" Honi inquired.
>
> "I am seventy years old today," replied the man.
>
> "Do you think that you will live to see this tree bear fruit?" asked Honi.
>
> The man replied, "When I came into the world, I found it full of mature carob trees. As my

> forebearers planted for me, so shall I plant for my children." (Talmud, *Ta'anit* 23a)

I hope that the teachings and practices in this book will help you to embrace aging, to live fully, joyfully, and bravely. May this be a time to learn and grow and also to teach, repair, and nurture. In this way, all that you have lived through can be harvested to nourish and inspire the future generations. I offer you this blessing for growing older:

> May you see the blessing in all your days,
> Notice beauty and sweetness, and be amazed.
> May you love without bound,
> Ever feel God surround.
> May you mend and tend,
> May you learn without end.
> May you see the blessing,
> May you seize the blessing,
> May you be a blessing in all your days.
>
> How many adventures you've had on your way
> Delights to be sure, also loss and dismay
> Your vision has broadened, your heart opened wide,
> Your wisdom deserves to be prized.
>
> May you see the blessing in all your days,
> Notice beauty and sweetness, and be amazed.
> May you love without bound,
> Ever feel God surround.

May you mend and tend,
May you learn without end.
May you see the blessing,
May you seize the blessing,
May you be a blessing in all your days.

You know now what counts, with the rest you are through,
You hold paradox and see gray, it is true.
No more playing safe, from your core you'll not veer,
Treasure this moment, it's dear.

—Words and melody by Rabbi Dayle A. Friedman (a recording can be found at http://growingolder.co/spiritual-resources/melodies-chants/a-blessing-for-growing-older)

Acknowledgments

This book is the fruit of several years of writing, but it is also the harvest of three decades of deeply satisfying work with elders. I am grateful to the elders of the Jewish Home and Hospital, the Philadelphia Geriatric Center, and Brith Sholom House, who were my early teachers about the terrain of later life. More recently, the brave and remarkable participants in my wisdom circles, the Wise Women and the Wise Guys, have taught me, shared their journeys with me, and served as early readers of much of the content of this volume.

I am indebted to Stuart M. Matlins, founder and publisher of Jewish Lights, and Emily Wichland, vice president of Editorial and Production at Jewish Lights, for encouragement, wise counsel, and most of all, for realizing my dream of sharing the riches of Jewish wisdom for those who are engaged in the adventure of growing older.

I have been accompanied in the process of writing this book by cherished guides and companions. I am grateful beyond measure to Mindy Brown, Julie Greenberg, and the members of my writing circle, Sonia Voynow, Sandy Kosmin, Linda Kriger, and Meredith Barber. Thank you for your invaluable inspiration, advice, and encouragement.

As this book took shape, our family endured tumult and transition—the loss of my mother-in-law, my brother-in-law, my father, and my sister; children's graduations and moves to high school and college; and a child's traumatic brain injury. I could not have gotten through these challenges, much less the exquisite agony of writing, were it not for all of my dear ones: the extended Ferleger, Freidman, and Marcus families; my Rosh Chodesh sisters, Beulah Trey, Irene McHenry, Lauren Pokras, Stacey Meadows, Shirley Brown, Sonia Voynow, and Joanne Buzaglo; and the "village" of precious friends who have again and again scooped me and my family up with love, care, and comfort.

Last, but truly first, everything I do is made possible by the foundation of love of my family: my beloved, David Ferleger, who embodies kindness and patience; and my children, Anya Friedman Hutter, Anat Friedman Ferleger, and Avram Friedman Ferleger, who teach me humility daily and give me hope for the future. I am blessed beyond measure.

APPENDIX

Using This Book

A Guide for Book Groups and Wisdom Circles

Book Groups

I strongly recommend that you share this book in the context of a group. The journey beyond midlife is rich and demanding. The quest to grow as we grow older requires support, encouragement, and sustenance. Sharing the exploration of the experience you are having and experimenting with the concepts, practices, and perspectives offered here can deepen your understanding and foster your growth. You can do this in a book group, where you can read the chapters together and try out the practices within them. You can reflect together on your reactions, including insights and also resistance that arises in relating to the material. You may want to address particular chapters of the book individually at sessions of your group.

Wisdom Circles

I also encourage you to consider sharing this book in the context of a wisdom circle. I have been leading wisdom circles with people beyond midlife for the past three years in Philadelphia. The idea behind a wisdom circle is to convene a context of safety, trust, and support for journeying together over time on the path beyond midlife. The educator Parker Palmer calls this kind of group a "circle of trust," and he suggests that being in such a community can be transformative for the self and those around us. The aim of a circle of trust, he teaches, is to empower each participant's shy soul to be able to be present and to speak its truth.[1] In the presence of nonjudgmental attention of the group, we can connect to our deepest longings and aspirations, to our authentic selves.

Convening a Wisdom Circle

The first step in convening a wisdom circle is to gather members. A good size for a group is between eight and twelve people. You can start with people you know—friends, neighbors, or acquaintances. It may be helpful for members to be from the same neighborhood or part of town. You can network to get an optimum number of people through social media, friends, and colleagues. I have found monthly meetings for two hours to be optimal. I would suggest at least a six-month commitment as a starting place. You can meet in members' homes or in a community space that is comfortable and private. It is a good idea to take turns bringing refreshments to share before and after the group.

Since your goal is to foster safety and ease, it is essential to agree on ground rules for the group. The most important rule is absolute confidentiality. What is shared in the wisdom circle stays in the wisdom circle. A second ground rule is about how members listen to one another. The central task is to hear one another into speech, as was often said in consciousness-raising groups in the 1960s. To do this, we need to stay out of each other's way, to make space for each person to uncover and share his or her truth. We have found it helpful to use this formulation from Parker Palmer: no fixing, no saving, no advising, no setting each other straight.[2]

A Suggested Structure for Wisdom Circle Meetings

You might seek a facilitator for your group—a social worker, clergyperson, therapist, or other professional. Alternatively, you can rotate leadership among members. The main role of the leader is to open and close the session, to keep to the time framework, and to monitor participation to make sure no one person dominates the conversations. Here is a brief outline of a structure for a two-hour session:

- Open with a poem, meditation, chant, or prayer. (5 minutes)
- Check-in: Each participant is invited to share a piece of wisdom he or she learned from a recent

experience—share the "nugget" of wisdom, without necessarily going into the story around it. (30 minutes)

- Discuss with one or two partners the material in the chapter (or a particular teaching within it) and your reactions—what is challenging, what is intriguing? If you like, you can read a text or passage aloud to one another to start. (20 minutes)
- Share highlights of this discussion with the whole group. (30 minutes)
- Try the practice outlined in the chapter and share reflections on how it was for you. (20 minutes)
- Close with a song, prayer, or poem. (5 minutes)
- Review logistics for the next session.

Reflect and Refine

However you choose to organize a group in which to share this exploration, it will be helpful to take time after two or so sessions to reflect on the experience. Are you getting what you'd hoped from it? Does the group feel safe and comfortable? Is there another way of working together that would be better for you? Discuss with one another, and refine your structure and approach as needed.

A Blessing

May your exploration of the journey beyond midlife renew, excite, and comfort you. May you open to learning and growth and to the others with whom you are sharing the way.

Notes

Introduction: Births Out of Brokenness

[1] Connie Goldman, *Who Am I ... Now That I'm Not Who I Was? Conversations with Women in Mid-life and the Years Beyond* (Minneapolis, MN: Nodin Press, 2009), 12.

[2] Elizabeth Lesser, *Broken Open: How Difficult Times Can Help Us Grow* (New York: Villard, 2005), 12.

[3] Richard Rohr, *Falling Upward: A Spirituality for the Two Halves of Life* (San Francisco: Jossey-Bass, 2011).

1. Seeking Wisdom: Transcending Destructive Ageism

[1] Mary Catherine Bateson, *Composing a Further Life: The Age of Active Wisdom* (New York: Knopf, 2010), 13–14.

[2] Marc Freedman, *Encore: Finding Work That Matters in the Second Half of Life* (New York: Public Affairs, 2007), 3–12.

[3] Sara Lawrence-Lightfoot, *The Third Chapter: Passion, Risk and Adventure in the 25 Years*

After 50 (New York: Sara Crichton Books, 2009), 4.

[4] William H. Thomas, *What Are Old People For? How Elders Will Save the World* (Acton, MA: VanderWyk & Burnham, 2007), 12–19.

[5] Margaret Morganroth Gullette, *Agewise: Fighting the New Ageism in America* (Chicago: University of Chicago Press, 2011), 24.

[6] Todd D. Nelson, quoted in ibid., 30.

[7] Quoted by William Safire, *New York Times Magazine,* August 20, 2006.

[8] Theodore Rozsak, *America the Wise: Longevity, Revolution and the True Wealth of Nations* (Boston: Houghton Mifflin, 1998), 107–109.

[9] James Hillman, *The Force of Character: And the Lasting Life* (New York: Ballantine Books, 2000), xx.

[10] Ronald Manheimer, "The Paradox of Beneficial Retirement: A Journey into the Vortex of Nothingness," *Journal of Aging, Humanities and the Arts* 2, no.2 (April 2008):93.

[11] Roszak, *America the Wise,* 221.

[12] Christopher Peterson and Martin Seligman, *Character Strengths and Virtues: A Handbook and Classification* (New York: Oxford University Press, 2004), 29.

[13] James Birren and Lauren Fisher, "The Elements of Wisdom: Overview and Integration," in *Wisdom: Its Nature, Origins, and Development,* ed. Robert Sternberg (Cambridge: Cambridge University Press, 1990), 324.

[14] Bateson, *Composing a Further Life,* 234.

[15] Robert Sternberg, *Why Smart People Can Be So Stupid* (New Haven, CT: Yale University Press, 2003), 235.

[16] Roszak, *America the Wise,* 230, 238.

2. One Big Hole: Confronting the Broken Heart

[1] Polly Young-Eisendrath, *Gifts of Suffering* (Reading, MA: Addison-Wesley, 1996), 59.

[2] Nancy Copeland-Payton, *The Losses of Our Lives: The Sacred Gifts of Renewal in Everyday Loss* (Woodstock, VT: SkyLight Paths, 2009), 151.

[3] Joan Chittister, *The Gift of Years: Growing Older Gracefully* (New York: BlueBridge, 2008), 91.

[4] My translation. For a melody with these words, see http://growingolder.co/spiritual-resources/melodies-chants.

3. The Ultimate Shattering: Embracing Our Mortality

[1] For a comprehensive review of Jewish approaches to life after death, see Simcha Paull Raphael, *Jewish Views of the Afterlife* (Lanham, MD: Rowman and Littlefield, 2009).

[2] Harold Schulweis, *Finding Each Other in Judaism: Meditations on the Rites of Passage from Birth to Immortality* (New York: URJ Press, 2001), 97.

[3] *Union Prayer Book* (New York: Central Conference of American Rabbis, 1940), 152.

[4] Stephen Levine, *A Year to Live: How to Live This Year as If It Were Your Last* (New York: Bell Tower, 1998), 75.

[5] Franz Kafka, *Diaries 1914–1923,* ed. Max Brod, trans. Martin Greenberg and Hannah Arendt (New York: Schocken Books, 1965), 195–96.

[6] Zalman Schachter-Shalomi and Ronald S. Miller, *From Age-ing to Sageing: A Profound New Vision of Growing Older* (New York: Warner Books, 1995), 87.

[7] Ibid., 103.

4. Finding Wholeness as Our Bodies Break Down

[1] Ram Dass, *Still Here: Embracing Aging, Changing, and Dying* (New York: Riverhead Books, 2000), 59.

[2] Ibid., 61.

5. Wandering in the Wilderness: Caring for Our Fragile Dear Ones

[1] Rosalynn Carter and Susan Golant, *Helping Yourself Help Others: A Book for Caregivers* (New York: Public Affairs, 2013), 1.

6. Making Sense of Dementia's Brokenness

[1] Anne Basting, *Forget Memory: Creating Better Lives for People with Dementia* (Baltimore: Johns Hopkins University Press, 2009), 7–11.

[2] Margaret Morganroth Gullette, *Agewise: Fighting the New Ageism in America* (Chicago: University of Chicago Press, 2011), 188.

[3] Rita Bresnahan, *Walking One Another Home: Moments of Grace and Possibility in the Midst of Alzheimer's* (Liguori, MO: Liguori, 2003), 82.

[4] Tom Kitwood, *Dementia Reconsidered: The Person Comes First* (Philadelphia: Open University Press, 1997).

[5] Bresnahan, *Walking One Another Home,* 110.

[6] Stephen Sapp, "'To See Things as God Sees Them': Theological Reflections on Pastoral Care to Persons with Dementia," in *Spiritual Care for Persons with Dementia: Fundamentals for Pastoral Practice,* ed. Larry VandeCreek (Binghamton, NY: Haworth Press, 1999), 37.

[7] Basting, *Forget Memory,* 18.

[8] Bresnahan, *Walking One Another Home,* 50.

[9] Susan H. McFadden and John T. McFadden, *Aging Together: Dementia, Friendship and Flourishing Communities* (Baltimore: Johns Hopkins University Press, 2011), 78.

[10] Ibid., 110.

[11] Diana Friel McGowin, *Living in the Labyrinth: A Personal Journey through the Maze of Alzheimer's* (New York: Delacorte Press, 1993), 14.

[12] Gullette, *Agewise,* 24.

7. Softening to Reality: Finding Sweetness amid Suffering

[1] Pema Chödrön, *The Places That Scare You: A Guide to Fearlessness in Difficult Times* (Boston: Shambhala, 2001), 25.

[2] Burt Jacobson, "Fear, Loss and the Power of Yielding," in *Seeking and Soaring: Jewish Approaches to Spiritual Guidance and Development,* ed. Goldie Milgram and Shohama Wiener (New York: Reclaiming Judaism Press, 2014), 303–14.

[3] William H. Thomas, *Second Wind: Navigating the Passage to a Slower, Deeper and More Connected Life* (New York: Simon and Schuster, 2014), 130.

8. A Time to Heal: Liberation through Forgiveness

[1] Rami Shapiro, personal communication. See Rami Shapiro, *Rabbi Rami Guide to Forgiveness: Roadside Assistance for the Spiritual Traveler* (Traverse City, MI: Spirituality & Health Books, 2011).

[2] The Intuition Network, *Thinking Allowed: Conversations on the Leading Edge of Knowledge*

and Discovery, television program with Dr. Jeffrey Mishlove, www.intuition.org.

[3] Melissa Dribben, "Grace amid the Losses," *Philadelphia Inquirer,* October 2, 2011.

[4] *Koren Sacks Siddur* (Jerusalem: Koren, 2009).

[5] Fred Luskin, *Forgive for Good: A Proven Prescription for Health and Happiness* (New York: HarperOne, 2003), 68, 74.

[6] Ibid., xiii.

[7] Ibid., 77–93.

9. Declaring Interdependence

[1] Jennie Keith, et al., *The Aging Experience: Diversity and Commonality across Cultures* (Thousand Oaks, CA: Sage, 1993), 258.

[2] Wendy Lustbader, *Counting on Kindness: The Dilemmas of Dependency* (New York: Free Press, 1994), 170–180.

[3] Abraham Joshua Heschel, "To Grow in Wisdom," in *The Insecurity of Freedom: Essays on Human Existence* (Philadelphia: Jewish Publication Society, 1966), 75.

[4] Maggie Kuhn, with Christina Long and Laura Quinn, *No Stone Unturned: The Life and Times of Maggie Kuhn* (New York: Ballantine Books, 1991), 228–29.

[5] Lustbader, *Counting on Kindness,* 168.

[6] Lawrence Kushner, *Honey from the Rock* (Woodstock, VT: Jewish Lights, 1990), 59–60.

10. Making Wise Choices about Medical Care at the Edge of Life

[1] Dennis McCullough, *My Mother, Your Mother: Embracing "Slow Medicine," the Compassionate Approach to Caring for Your Aging Loved Ones* (New York: Harper, 2008), 49.

[2] Sharon R. Kaufman, Janet K. Shim, and Ann J. Russ, "Revisiting the Biomedicalization of Aging: Clinical Trends and Ethical Challenges," *Gerontologist* 44, no.6 (2004):737.

[3] The Conversation Project is a wonderful resource, offering a user-friendly guide for preparing for and having conversations with those close to us about our wishes regarding end-of-life care: www.theconversationproject.org.

11. New Ways of Loving: Growing Up as We and Our Parents Age

[1] Vivian Greenberg, *Children of a Certain Age* (New York: Lexington Books, 1994), 12.

[2] Ibid., 31.

[3] Ibid., 21.

[4] Virginia Morris, *How to Care for Your Aging Parents* (New York: Workman Press, 1996), 36.

[5] Greenberg, *Children of a Certain Age,* 60.

[6] Ibid., 54.

[7] Morris, *How to Care for Your Aging Parents,* 21.

12. Traveling Lighter: Winnowing "Stuff"

[1] *Pirke Avot* 2:7, my translation. *Basar,* translated as "flesh," could also be rendered "meat," which comports with the notion of consumption.

[2] Joan Chittister, *The Gift of Years: Growing Older Gracefully* (New York: BlueBridge, 2008), 91.

[3] Menachem Mendel of Satanov, *Heshbon HaNefesh,* trans. Dovid Landesman (New York: Feldheim, 2005), 128.

13. A Sanctuary in Time: Spending Our Precious Time Mindfully

[1] Sholom Noach Berezovsky, *Netivot Shalom* on *Hayyei Sarah, Ba bayamim,* my translation.

[2] William H. Thomas, *Second Wind: Navigating the Passage to a Slower, Deeper, and More Connected Life* (New York: Simon and Schuster, 2014), 198.

[3] Florida Scott-Maxwell, *The Measure of My Days* (New York: Penguin Books, 1979), 41.

[4] Abraham Joshua Heschel, "To Grow in Wisdom," in *The Insecurity of Freedom: Essays on Human Existence* (Philadelphia: Jewish Publication Society, 1966), 82.

14. Answering the Call: Saying "Here I Am" (Hineini)

[1] Abraham Joshua Heschel, "To Grow in Wisdom," in *The Insecurity of Freedom: Essays on Human Existence* (Philadelphia: Jewish Publication Society, 1966), 74.

[2] Sara Lawrence-Lightfoot, *The Third Chapter: Passion, Risk and Adventure in the 25 Years After 50* (New York: Sarah Crichton Press, 2009), 244.

[3] Heschel, "To Grow in Wisdom," 78.

[4] Mary Catherine Bateson, *Composing a Further Life: The Age of Active Wisdom* (New York: Knopf, 2010), 13–14.

[5] Lightfoot-Lawrence, *The Third Chapter,* 105–140.

[6] Marc Freedman, *The Big Shift: Navigating the New State Beyond Midlife* (New York: Public Affairs, 2011), 5.

[7] Michael Vitez, "Phila. Granny Brigade Wages Peace," *Philadelphia Inquirer,* Sept. 16, 2013, http://articles.philly.com/2013-09-16/news/42083528_1_goldie-petkov-flier-grannies.

[8] Marc Freedman, *The Big Shift,* 130–140.

[9] Maggie Kuhn, with Christina Long and Laura Quinn, *No Stone Unturned: The Life and Times of Maggie Kuhn* (New York: Ballantine Books, 1991), 212–13.

15. Drawing from the Well: Developing a Blessing Practice

[1] Rabbi Yael Levy, interpretation offered at "A Way In" meditation service, Mishkan Shalom Congregation, Philadelphia, PA.

[2] Brene Brown, *Daring Greatly: How the Courage to be Vulnerable Transforms the Way We Live, Love, Parent, and Lead* (New York: Gotham Books, 2012), 87.

[3] Sonja Lyubomirsky, *The How of Happiness: A New Approach to Getting the Life You Want* (New York: Penguin Press, 2007), 90.

[4] Robert Emmons, *Thanks! How the New Science of Gratitude Can Make You Happier* (Boston: Houghton Mifflin, 2007), 30.

[5] Cited by Alan Morinis, *Everyday Holiness: The Jewish Spiritual Path of Mussar* (Boston: Trumpeter, 2008), 65.

[6] For more on this practice, see Sharon Salzburg, *Lovingkindness: The Revolutionary Art of Happiness* (Boston: Shambhala Classics, 1995).

[7] David Spangler, *Blessing: The Art and the Practice* (New York: Riverhead Books, 2001), 7.

Appendix: Using This Book

[1] Parker Palmer, *A Hidden Wholeness: The Journey toward an Undivided Life* (San Francisco: Jossey-Bass, 2009), 45.

[2] Ibid., 115.

For Further Learning

Books

Address, Richard F., ed. *A Time to Prepare.* New York: URJ Press, 2002.

Address, Richard A., and Hara E. Person, eds. *That You May Live Long: Caring for our Aging Parents, Caring for Ourselves.* New York: URJ Press, 2003.

Basting, Anne. *Forget Memory: Creating Better Lives for People with Dementia.* Baltimore: Johns Hopkins University Press, 2009.

Bateson, Mary Catherine. *Composing a Further Life: The Age of Active Wisdom.* New York: Knopf, 2010.

Brenner, Daniel S., Tsvi Blanchard, Joseph Fins, and Bradley Hirschfield. *Embracing Life and Facing Death: A Jewish Guide to Palliative Care.* New York: CLAL, 2002.

Bresnahan, Rita. *Walking One Another Home: Moments of Grace and Possibility in the Midst of Alzheimer's.* Liguori, MO: Liguori, 2003.

Chittister, Joan. *The Gift of Years.* New York: BlueBridge, 2008.

Copeland-Payton, Nancy. *The Losses of Our Lives.* Woodstock, VT: SkyLight Paths, 2009.

Dickstein, Stephanie. *With Sweetness from the Rock: A Jewish Spiritual Companion for Caregivers.* New York: National Center for Jewish Healing. www.ncjh.org.

Dorff, Eliot. *Matters of Life and Death: A Jewish Approach to Modern Medical Ethics.* Philadelphia: Jewish Publication Society, 2004.

Eilberg, Amy. "Walking in the Valley of the Shadow: Caring for the Dying and Their Loved Ones." In *Jewish Pastoral Care: A Practical Handbook from Traditional and Contemporary Sources,* edited by Dayle A. Friedman. 2nd ed. Woodstock, VT: Jewish Lights, 2010.

Emmons, Robert. *Thanks! How the New Science of Gratitude Can Make You Happier.* Boston: Houghton Mifflin, 2007.

Freedman, Marc. *The Big Shift: Navigating the New Stage beyond Midlife.* New York: Public Affairs, 2011.

Friedman, Dayle A., ed. *Jewish Pastoral Care: A Practical Handbook from Traditional & Contemporary Sources.* 2nd ed. Woodstock, VT: Jewish Lights, 2005.

_____. *Jewish Visions for Aging: A Professional Guide for Fostering Wholeness.* Woodstock, VT: Jewish Lights, 2008.

Greenberg, Vivian. *Children of a Certain Age.* New York: Lexington Books, 1994.

Gullette, Margaret Morganroth. *Agewise: Fighting the New Ageism in America.* Chicago: University of Chicago Press, 2011.

Heschel, Abraham Joshua. "To Grow in Wisdom." In *The Insecurity of Freedom: Essays on Human Existence.* Philadelphia: Jewish Publication Society, 1966.

Jacobs, Barry. *The Emotional Survival Guide for Family Caregivers: Looking After Yourself and Your Family While Helping an Aging Parent.* New York: Guilford Press, 2006.

Kuhn, Maggie, with Christina Long and Laura Quinn. *No Stone Unturned: The Life and Times of Maggie Kuhn.* New York: Ballantine Books, 1991.

Lawrence-Lightfoot, Sara. *The Third Chapter: Passion, Risk and Adventure in the 25 Years After 50.* New York: Sarah Crichton Press, 2009.

Levine, Stephen. *A Year to Live: How to Live This Year as If It Were Your Last.* New York: Bell Tower, 1998.

Lew, Alan. *Be Still and Get Going: A Jewish Meditation Practice for Real Life.* New York: Little, Brown, 2005.

Luskin, Fred. *Forgive for Good: A Proven Prescription for Health and Happiness.* New York: HarperOne, 2003.

Lustbader, Wendy. *Counting on Kindness: The Dilemmas of Dependency.* New York: Free Press, 1993.

Mace, Nancy, and Peter Rabins. *The 36-Hour Day: A Family Guide to Caring for Persons with Alzheimer's Disease, Related Dementing Illnesses and Memory Loss in Later Life.* 5th ed. New York: Grand Central Life and Style, 2012.

McCullough, Dennis. *My Mother, Your Mother: Embracing "Slow Medicine," the Compassionate Approach to Caring for Your Aging Loved Ones.* New York: Harper, 2008.

McFadden, Susan H., and John T. McFadden. *Aging Together: Dementia, Friendship and Flourishing Communities.* Baltimore: Johns Hopkins University Press, 2011.

McGowin, Diana Friel. *Living in the Labyrinth: A Personal Journey through the Maze of Alzheimer's.* New York: Delacorte Press, 1993.

Menachem Mendel of Satanov. *Cheshbon HaNefesh.* Translated by Dovid Landesman. New York: Feldheim, 2005.

Morris, Virginia. *How to Care for Aging Parents.* New York: Workman, 1996.

Palmer, Parker. *A Hidden Wholeness: The Journey toward an Undivided Life.* San Francisco: Jossey-Bass, 2009.

Ram Dass. *Still Here: Embracing Aging, Changing, and Dying.* New York: Riverhead Books, 2000.

Raphael, Simcha Paull. *Jewish Views of the Afterlife.* Lanham, MD: Rowman and Littlefield, 2009.

Rohr, Richard. *Falling Upward: A Spirituality for the Two Halves of Life.* San Francisco: Jossey-Bass, 2011.

Roszak, Theodore. *America the Wise: The Longevity Revolution and the True Wealth of Nations.* Boston: Houghton Mifflin, 1998.

Roth, Jeff. *Jewish Meditation Practices for Everyday Life: Awakening Your Heart, Connecting with God.* Woodstock, VT: Jewish Lights, 2011.

Schachter-Shalomi, Zalman, and Ronald Miller. *From Age-ing to Sage-ing.* New York: Warner Books, 1997.

Scott-Maxwell, Florida. *The Measure of My Days.* New York: Penguin Books, 1979.

Thomas, Bill. *Second Wind: Navigating the Passage to a Slower, Deeper, and More Connected Life.* New York: Simon and Schuster, 2014.

Thomas, William H. *What Are Old People For? How Elders Will Save the World.* Acton, MA: VanderWyk & Burnham, 2007.

Other Useful Resources

AARP Caregiving Resource, www.aarp.org/content/aarp/en/home/relationships/caregiving.html: offers helpful tools, worksheets, and tips for caregivers

Awakened Heart Project, www.awakenedheart.org: offers retreats to teach Jewish meditation

Caring Connections, www.caringinfo.org/i4a/pages/index.cfm?pageid=3289: offers state-specific advance directive forms

The Conversation Project, www.theconversationproject.org: offers a user-friendly guide for preparing for and having conversations with those close to us about our wishes regarding end-of-life care

Family Caregiver Alliance (FCA), www.caregiver.org/caregiver: addresses needs of family members and others providing long-term care at home

Five Wishes Guide on Advance Care Planning, www.agingwithdignity.org/fivewishes.php: helpful document to articulate wishes, goals, and concerns about end-of-life care

Dayle A. Friedman, Growing Older website, http://growingolder.co/spiritualresources/melodies-chants: recording of melodies for *Modah Ani,* loving-kindness blessings, and blessing for growing older

Institute for Jewish Spirituality, 135 West 29th Street, Suite 1103, New York, NY 10001-5224, 646-461-6499, www.jewishspirituality.org: offers audio and video recordings of meditation and yoga practices; teaches Jewish contemplative spiritual practices

My Gift of Grace, http://mygiftofgrace.com: game that facilitates conversations about living and dying for families or small groups

AVAILABLE FROM BETTER BOOKSTORES. TRY YOUR BOOKSTORE FIRST.

Bible Study / Midrash

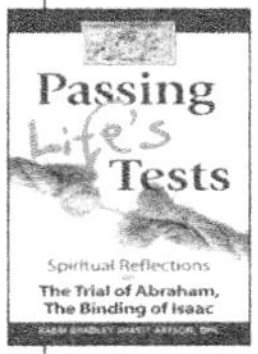

Passing Life's Tests: Spiritual Reflections on the Trial of Abraham, the Binding of Isaac *By Rabbi Bradley Shavit Artson, DHL*
Invites us to use this powerful tale as a tool for our own soul wrestling, to confront our existential sacrifices and enable us to face—and surmount—life's tests.

Speaking Torah: Spiritual Teachings from around the Maggid's Table—in Two Volumes *By Arthur Green, with Ebn Leader, Ariel Evan Mayse and Or N. Rose*
The most powerful Hasidic teachings made accessible—from some of the world's preeminent authorities on Jewish thought and spirituality.
Volume 1
Volume 2

A Partner in Holiness: Deepening Mindfulness, Practicing Compassion and Enriching Our Lives through the Wisdom of R. Levi Yitzhak of Berdichev's *Kedushat Levi*
By Rabbi Jonathan P. Slater, DMin; Foreword by Arthur Green; Preface by Rabby Nancy Flam
Contemporary mindfulness and classical Hasidic spirituality are brought together to inspire a satisfying spiritual life of practice.
Volume 1
Volume 2

The Genesis of Leadership: What the Bible Teaches Us about Vision, Values and Leading Change *By Rabbi Nathan Laufer; Foreword by Senator Joseph I. Lieberman*

Hineini in Our Lives
Learning How to Respond to Others through 14 Biblical Texts and Personal Stories
By Dr. Norman J. Cohen

Masking and Unmasking Ourselves: Interpreting Biblical Texts on Clothing & Identity *By Dr. Norman J. Cohen*

The Messiah and the Jews: Three Thousand Years of Tradition, Belief and Hope
By Rabbi Elaine Rose Glickman; Foreword by Rabbi Neil Gillman, PhD
Preface by Rabbi Judith Z. Abrams, PhD

The Modern Men's Torah Commentary: New Insights from Jewish Men on the 54 Weekly Torah Portions *Edited by Rabbi Jeffrey K. Salkin*

Moses and the Journey to Leadership: Timeless Lessons of Effective Management from the Bible and Today's Leaders *By Dr. Norman J. Cohen*

The Other Talmud—The *Yerushalmi*: Unlocking the Secrets of *The Talmud of Israel* for Judaism Today *By Rabbi Judith Z. Abrams, PhD*

Sage Tales: Wisdom and Wonder from the Rabbis of the Talmud
By Rabbi Burton L. Visotzky

The Torah Revolution: Fourteen Truths That Changed the World
By Rabbi Reuven Hammer, PhD

The Wisdom of Judaism: An Introduction to the Values of the Talmud
By Rabbi Dov Peretz Elkins

Or phone, fax, mail or email to: **JEWISH LIGHTS Publishing**
Sunset Farm Offices, Route 4 • P.O. Box 237 • Woodstock, Vermont 05091
Tel: (802) 457-4000 • Fax: (802) 457-4004 • www.jewishlights.com
Credit card orders: (800) 962-4544 (8:30AM–5:30PM EST Monday–Friday)
Generous discounts on quantity orders. SATISFACTION GUARANTEED. Prices subject to change.

Children's Books

Lullaby
By Debbie Friedman; Full-color illus. by Lorraine Bubar
A charming adaptation of beloved singer-songwriter Debbie Friedman's best-selling song *Lullaby*, this timeless bedtime picture book will help children know that God will keep them safe throughout the night.
9 x 12, 32 pp, Full-color illus., w/ a CD of original music & lyrics by Debbie Friedman
For ages 3–6

Around the World in One Shabbat
Jewish People Celebrate the Sabbath Together
By Durga Yael Bernhard
Takes your child on a colorful adventure to share the many ways Jewish people celebrate Shabbat around the world.
For ages 3–6

It's a ... It's a ... It's a Mitzvah
By Liz Suneby and Diane Heiman; Full-color illus. by Laurel Molk
Join Mitzvah Meerkat and friends as they introduce children to the everyday kindnesses that mark the beginning of a Jewish journey and a lifetime commitment to *tikkun olam* (repairing the world).
For ages 3–6

Also available as a Board Book: **That's a Mitzvah**
For ages 1–4

What You Will See Inside a Synagogue
By Rabbi Lawrence A. Hoffman, PhD, and Dr. Ron Wolfson; Full-color photos by Bill Aron
A colorful, fun-to-read introduction that explains the ways and whys of Jewish worship and religious life.
For ages 6 & up

Because Nothing Looks Like God
By Lawrence Kushner and Karen Kushner
Invites parents and children to explore, together, the questions we all have about God.
For ages 4 & up

In God's Hands *By Lawrence Kushner and Gary Schmidt*
Each of us has the power to make the world a better place—working ordinary miracles with our everyday deeds.
For ages 5 & up

What Makes Someone a Jew? *By Lauren Seidman*
Reflects the changing face of American Judaism. Helps preschoolers and young readers understand that you don't have to look a certain way to be Jewish.
For ages 3–6

In Our Image: God's First Creatures
By Nancy Sohn Swartz God asks all of nature to offer gifts to humankind—with a promise that the humans would care for creation in return.
For ages 5 & up
Animated app available on Apple App Store and the Google Play Marketplace

The Book of Miracles: A Young Person's Guide to Jewish Spiritual Awareness
Written and illus. by Lawrence Kushner
For ages 9–13

The Jewish Family Fun Book, 2nd Edition: Holiday Projects, Everyday Activities, and Travel Ideas with Jewish Themes *By Danielle Dardashti and Roni Sarig*

When a Grandparent Dies: A Kid's Own Remembering Workbook for Dealing with Shiva and the Year Beyond *By Nechama Liss-Levinson*
For ages 7–13

**A book from SkyLight Paths, Jewish Lights' sister imprint*

Children's Books by Sandy Eisenberg Sasso

The *Shema* in the Mezuzah
Listening to Each Other
Introduces children ages 3 to 6 to the words of the *Shema* and the custom of putting up the mezuzah. Winner, National Jewish Book Award.
For ages 3–6

Adam & Eve's First Sunset
God's New Day
Explores fear and hope, faith and gratitude in ways that will delight kids and adults—inspiring us to bless each of God's days and nights.
For ages 4 & up

Also Available as a Board Book: **Adam and Eve's New Day**
For ages 1–4

But God Remembered
Stories of Women from Creation to the Promised Land
Four different stories of women—Lilith, Serach, Bityah and the Daughters of Z—teach us important values through their faith and actions.
For ages 8 & up

For Heaven's Sake
Heaven is often found where you least expect it.
For ages 4 & up

God Said Amen
An inspiring story about hearing the answers to our prayers.
For ages 4 & up

God's Paintbrush: Special 10th Anniversary Edition
Wonderfully interactive, invites children of all faiths and backgrounds to encounter God through moments in their own lives. Provides questions adult and child can explore together.
For ages 4 & up

Also Available as a Board Book: **I Am God's Paintbrush**
For ages 1–4

Also Available: **God's Paintbrush Teacher's Guide**

God's Paintbrush Celebration Kit:
A Spiritual Activity Kit for Teachers and Students of All Faiths, All Backgrounds

In God's Name
Like an ancient myth in its poetic text and vibrant illustrations, this award-winning modern fable about the search for God's name celebrates the diversity and, at the same time, the unity of all people.
For ages 4 & up

Also Available as a Board Book: **What Is God's Name?**
For ages 1–4

Also Available in Spanish: **El nombre de Dios**
For ages 4 & up

Noah's Wife
The Story of Naamah
When God tells Noah to bring the animals of the world onto the ark, God also calls on Naamah, Noah's wife, to save each plant on earth.
For ages 4 & up

Also Available as a Board Book: **Naamah, Noah's Wife**
For ages 1–4

**A book from SkyLight Paths, Jewish Lights' sister imprint*

Social Justice

Where Justice Dwells
A Hands-On Guide to Doing Social Justice in Your Jewish Community
By Rabbi Jill Jacobs; Foreword by Rabbi David Saperstein
Provides ways to envision and act on your own ideals of social justice.

There Shall Be No Needy
Pursuing Social Justice through Jewish Law and Tradition
By Rabbi Jill Jacobs; Foreword by Rabbi Elliot N. Dorff, PhD; Preface by Simon Greer
Confronts the most pressing issues of twenty-first-century America from a deeply Jewish perspective.

There Shall Be No Needy Teacher's Guide

Conscience
The Duty to Obey and the Duty to Disobey
By Rabbi Harold M. Schulweis
Examines the idea of conscience and the role conscience plays in our relationships to government, law, ethics, religion, human nature, God—and to each other.

Judaism and Justice: The Jewish Passion to Repair the World
By Rabbi Sidney Schwarz; Foreword by Ruth Messinger

Spirituality / Women's Interest

Embracing the Divine Feminine: Finding God through the Ecstasy of Physical Love—The Song of Songs Annotated & Explained
Annotation and Translation by Rabbi Rami Shapiro; Foreword by Rev. Cynthia Bourgeault, PhD
Restores the Song of Songs' eroticism and interprets it as a celebration of the love between the Divine Feminine and the contemporary spiritual seeker.

The Women's Haftarah Commentary
New Insights from Women Rabbis on the 54 Weekly Haftarah Portions, the 5 Megillot & Special Shabbatot
Edited by Rabbi Elyse Goldstein
Illuminates the historical significance of female portrayals in the Haftarah and the Five Megillot.

The Women's Torah Commentary
New Insights from Women Rabbis on the 54 Weekly Torah Portions
Edited by Rabbi Elyse Goldstein
Over fifty women rabbis offer inspiring insights on the Torah, in a week-by-week format.

The Divine Feminine in Biblical Wisdom Literature
Selections Annotated & Explained
Translation & Annotation by Rabbi Rami Shapiro; Foreword by Rev. Cynthia Bourgeault, PhD

New Jewish Feminism: Probing the Past, Forging the Future
Edited by Rabbi Elyse Goldstein; Foreword by Anita Diamant

The Quotable Jewish Woman
Wisdom, Inspiration & Humor from the Mind & Heart
Edited by Elaine Bernstein Partnow

See Passover for *The Women's Passover Companion: Women's Reflections on the Festival of Freedom* and *The Women's Seder Sourcebook: Rituals & Readings for Use at the Passover Seder.*

**A book from SkyLight Paths, Jewish Lights' sister imprint*

Meditation / Yoga

Living the Life of Jewish Meditation: A Comprehensive Guide to Practice and Experience *By Rabbi Yoel Glick*
Combines the knowledge of Judaism with the spiritual practice of Yoga to lead you to an encounter with your true self. Includes nineteen different meditations.

***Mussar* Yoga:** Blending an Ancient Jewish Spiritual Practice with Yoga to Transform Body and Soul
By Edith R. Brotman, PhD, RYT-500; Foreword by Alan Morinis
A clear and easy-to-use introduction to an embodied spiritual practice for anyone seeking profound and lasting self-transformation.

The Magic of Hebrew Chant: Healing the Spirit, Transforming the Mind, Deepening Love
By Rabbi Shefa Gold; Foreword by Sylvia Boorstein
Introduces this transformative spiritual practice as a way to unlock the power of sacred texts and make prayer and meditation the delight of your life. Includes musical notations.

Ritual / Sacred Practices

The Rituals & Practices of a Jewish Life: A Handbook for Personal Spiritual Renewal
Edited by Rabbi Kerry M. Olitzky and Rabbi Daniel Judson

The Sacred Art of Lovingkindness: Preparing to Practice
By Rabbi Rami Shapiro

Grief / Healing

Facing Illness, Finding God: How Judaism Can Help You and Caregivers Cope When Body or Spirit Fails *By Rabbi Joseph B. Meszler*

Grief in Our Seasons: A Mourner's Kaddish Companion *By Rabbi Kerry M. Olitzky*

Healing and the Jewish Imagination: Spiritual and Practical Perspectives on Judaism and Health *Edited by Rabbi William Cutter, PhD*

Healing from Despair: Choosing Wholeness in a Broken World
By Rabbi Elie Kaplan Spitz with Erica Shapiro Taylor; Foreword by Abraham J. Twerski, MD

Healing of Soul, Healing of Body: Spiritual Leaders Unfold the Strength & Solace in Psalms *Edited by Rabbi Simkha Y. Weintraub, LCSW*

Midrash & Medicine: Healing Body and Soul in the Jewish Interpretive Tradition
Edited by Rabbi William Cutter, PhD; Foreword by Michele F. Prince, LCSW, MAJCS

Mourning & Mitzvah, 2nd Edition: A Guided Journal for Walking the Mourner's Path through Grief to Healing *By Rabbi Anne Brener, LCSW*

A Time to Mourn, a Time to Comfort, 2nd Edition
A Guide to Jewish Bereavement *By Dr. Ron Wolfson; Foreword by Rabbi David J. Wolpe*

When a Grandparent Dies: A Kid's Own Remembering Workbook for Dealing with Shiva and the Year Beyond *By Nechama Liss-Levinson, PhD*
For ages 7–13

**A book from SkyLight Paths, Jewish Lights' sister imprint*

Inspiration

The Chutzpah Imperative: Empowering Today's Jews for a Life That Matters *By Rabbi Edward Feinstein; Foreword by Rabbi Laura Geller*
A new view of chutzpah as Jewish self-empowerment to be God's partner and repair the world. Reveals Judaism's ancient message, its deepest purpose and most precious treasures.

Judaism's Ten Best Ideas: A Brief Guide for Seekers
By Rabbi Arthur Green, PhD A highly accessible introduction to Judaism's greatest contributions to civilization, drawing on Jewish mystical tradition and the author's experience.

Into the Fullness of the Void: A Spiritual Autobiography *By Dov Elbaum*
One of Israel's leading cultural figures provides insights and guidance for all of us.

The Bridge to Forgiveness: Stories and Prayers for Finding God and Restoring Wholeness
By Rabbi Karyn D. Kedar

The Empty Chair: Finding Hope and Joy—Timeless Wisdom from a Hasidic Master, Rebbe Nachman of Breslov *Adapted by Moshe Mykoff and the Breslov Research Institute*

The Gentle Weapon: Prayers for Everyday and Not-So-Everyday Moments—Timeless Wisdom from the Teachings of the Hasidic Master Rebbe Nachman of Breslov
Adapted by Moshe Mykoff and S. C. Mizrahi, together with the Breslov Research Institute

God Whispers: Stories of the Soul, Lessons of the Heart *By Rabbi Karyn D. Kedar*

God's To-Do List: 103 Ways to Be an Angel and Do God's Work on Earth
By Dr. Ron Wolfson

Happiness and the Human Spirit: The Spirituality of Becoming the Best You Can Be
By Rabbi Abraham J. Twerski, MD

Life's Daily Blessings: Inspiring Reflections on Gratitude and Joy for Every Day, Based on Jewish Wisdom *By Rabbi Kerry M. Olitzky*

Restful Reflections: Nighttime Inspiration to Calm the Soul, Based on Jewish Wisdom
By Rabbi Kerry M. Olitzky and Rabbi Lori Forman-Jacobi

Sacred Intentions: Morning Inspiration to Strengthen the Spirit, Based on Jewish Wisdom
By Rabbi Kerry M. Olitzky and Rabbi Lori Forman-Jacobi

Saying No and Letting Go: Jewish Wisdom on Making Room for What Matters Most
By Rabbi Edwin Goldberg, DHL; Foreword by Rabbi Naomi Levy

The Seven Questions You're Asked in Heaven: Reviewing and Renewing Your Life on Earth *By Dr. Ron Wolfson*

Kabbalah / Mysticism

Ehyeh: A Kabbalah for Tomorrow
By Rabbi Arthur Green, PhD

The Gift of Kabbalah: Discovering the Secrets of Heaven, Renewing Your Life on Earth
By Tamar Frankiel, PhD

Jewish Mysticism and the Spiritual Life: Classical Texts, Contemporary Reflections *Edited by Dr. Lawrence Fine, Dr. Eitan Fishbane and Rabbi Or N. Rose*

Seek My Face: A Jewish Mystical Theology *By Rabbi Arthur Green, PhD*

Zohar: Annotated & Explained *Translation & Annotation by Dr. Daniel C. Matt*
Foreword by Andrew Harvey
(A book from SkyLight Paths, Jewish Lights' sister imprint)

Spirituality

Amazing *Chesed*: Living a Grace-Filled Judaism
By Rabbi Rami Shapiro Drawing from ancient and contemporary, traditional and non-traditional Jewish wisdom, reclaims the idea of grace in Judaism.

Jewish with Feeling: A Guide to Meaningful Jewish Practice
By Rabbi Zalman Schachter-Shalomi (z"l) with Joel Segel
Takes off from basic questions like "Why be Jewish?" and whether the word *God* still speaks to us today and lays out a vision for a whole-person Judaism.

Perennial Wisdom for the Spiritually Independent: Sacred Teachings—Annotated & Explained *Annotation by Rabbi Rami Shapiro; Foreword by Richard Rohr*
Weaves sacred texts and teachings from the world's major religions into a coherent exploration of the five core questions at the heart of every religion's search.

A Book of Life: Embracing Judaism as a Spiritual Practice
By Rabbi Michael Strassfeld

Bringing the Psalms to Life: How to Understand and Use the Book of Psalms
By Rabbi Daniel F. Polish, PhD

Does the Soul Survive? 2nd Edition: A Jewish Journey to Belief in Afterlife, Past Lives & Living with Purpose *By Rabbi Elie Kaplan Spitz; Foreword by Brian L. Weiss, MD*

Entering the Temple of Dreams: Jewish Prayers, Movements and Meditations for the End of the Day *By Tamar Frankiel, PhD, and Judy Greenfeld*

First Steps to a New Jewish Spirit: Reb Zalman's Guide to Recapturing the Intimacy & Ecstasy in Your Relationship with God
By Rabbi Zalman Schachter-Shalomi (z"l) with Donald Gropman

Foundations of Sephardic Spirituality: The Inner Life of Jews of the Ottoman Empire
By Rabbi Marc D. Angel, PhD

God & the Big Bang: Discovering Harmony between Science & Spirituality
By Dr. Daniel C. Matt

God in Our Relationships: Spirituality between People from the Teachings of Martin Buber
By Rabbi Dennis S. Ross

The God Upgrade: Finding Your 21st-Century Spirituality in Judaism's 5,000-Year-Old Tradition *By Rabbi Jamie Korngold; Foreword by Rabbi Harold M. Schulweis*

The Jewish Lights Spirituality Handbook: A Guide to Understanding, Exploring & Living a Spiritual Life *Edited by Stuart M. Matlins*

Judaism, Physics and God: Searching for Sacred Metaphors in a Post-Einstein World
By Rabbi David W. Nelson

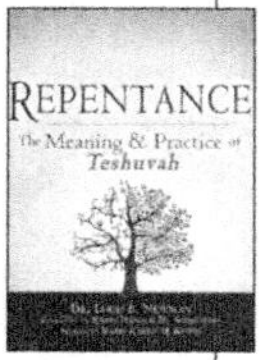

Repentance: The Meaning and Practice of Teshuvah
By Dr. Louis E. Newman; Foreword by Rabbi Harold M. Schulweis; Preface by Rabbi Karyn D. Kedar

The Sabbath Soul: Mystical Reflections on the Transformative Power of Holy Time
Selection, Translation and Commentary by Eitan Fishbane, PhD

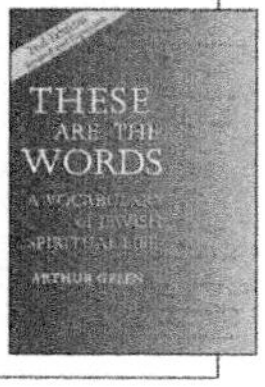

***Tanya*, the Masterpiece of Hasidic Wisdom:** Selections Annotated & Explained
Translation & Annotation by Rabbi Rami Shapiro; Foreword by Rabbi Zalman Schachter-Shalomi (z"l)

These Are the Words, 2nd Edition: A Vocabulary of Jewish Spiritual Life
By Rabbi Arthur Green, PhD

The path of aging isn't easy—wise guidance and supportive practices can help you make the most of the journey.

> "The journey beyond midlife is not a straightforward trip but rather an unfolding path full of twists and turns, of shocking surprises and, if we are open, perhaps unexpected delights. We cannot plan this journey; we simply cannot anticipate when and how our health will challenge us.... We need guidance to find our way with resilience, courage and blessing."
>
> *—from the Introduction*

Rabbi, chaplain, teacher and spiritual leader Dayle Friedman helps us find our way to wholeness in this unprecedented swath of life. With gentle guidance, she helps us explore:

- **The Shatterings—**the changes and challenges that confront us as we grow older
- **The Sparks—**the new beginnings that can take place in the wake of loss and limits
- **The Light of Wisdom—**the ways we hone and share our wisdom by living fully and generously

For anyone in midlife, caring for aging loved ones, or in healthcare or social service professions, the spiritual sustenance you will find here will inspire you to find radiance and resilience on the complex journey of growing older.

> "Fearless and truthful.... [It] looks without flinching at grief and all the 'shatterings' of later life yet ... finds joy and a realistic hope.... This is a book to reach for whenever you want inspiration, whenever you seek to live each day as it comes. Don't miss this book."
>
> **—Harry R. Moody,** retired vice president, AARP; visiting professor, Creative Longevity and Wisdom Program, Fielding Graduate Universityy

Also Available

The Seven Questions You're Asked in Heaven
Reviewing & Renewing Your Life on Earth

By Dr. Ron Wolfson
Provides an advance copy of the Seven Questions you'll be asked in heaven—whether you're a believer or a non-believer—to help you shape a life of purpose and meaning on earth today.

Caresharing

A Reciprocal Approach to Caregiving and Care Receiving in the Complexities of Aging, Illness or Disability

By Marty Richards

Shows you how to move from independent caregiving to interdependent caregiving by engaging the spiritual and emotional aspects of caring for a loved one.

A book from SkyLight Paths, Jewish Lights' sister imprint

Rabbi Dayle A. Friedman, MSW, MA, BCC, is a pioneer in forging a fresh vision for the second half of life. She is a spiritual leader, social innovator, scholar, author of *Jewish Visions for Aging: A Professional Guide to Fostering Wholeness* and editor of *Jewish Pastoral Care: A Practical Handbook from Traditional and Contemporary Sources.* She founded and directed Hiddur: The Center for Aging and Judaism of the Reconstructionist Rabbinical College. Rabbi Friedman offers training, consulting and spiritual guidance through Growing Older (www.growingolder.co), her Philadelphia-based national practice.

Rabbi Friedman is available to speak to your group or at your event. For more information, please contact us at (802)457-4000 or publicity@jewishlights.com.

***

"How enlightening and compassionate this book is! This is the kind of wisdom we need in any religion, in any culture and in any age of life."

—Fr. Richard Rohr, OFM, Center for Action and Contemplation, Albuquerque, New Mexico

"A great gift.... Gives us hope that we can have happiness and well-being almost independently of what's happening with our bodies. Thank you, Rabbi Friedman, from someone who is well beyond midlife!"

—Daniel Gottlieb, PhD, psychologist and family therapist; host, Voices in the Family WHYY FM; author, *The Wisdom We're Born With: Restoring Our Faith in Ourselves*

"Rabbi Friedman writes with remarkable tenderness and uncommon empathy about the gifts, challenges and epiphanies of aging.... Her book doesn't just offer blessings, it is itself a blessing."

—Letty Cottin Pogrebin, author, *Getting Over Getting Older* and *Single Jewish Male Seeking Soulmate*

Also Available from Rabbi Dayle A. Friedman

Jewish Visions for Aging
A Professional Guide for Fostering Wholenesss

By Rabbi Dayle A. Friedman, MSW, MAJCS, BCC
Foreword by Thomas R. Cole, PhD; Preface by Dr. Eugene B. Borowitz

This rich resource probes Jewish texts, spirituality and observance, uncovering a deep, never-before-realized approach to responding to the challenges of aging with a refreshing and inspiring vitality.

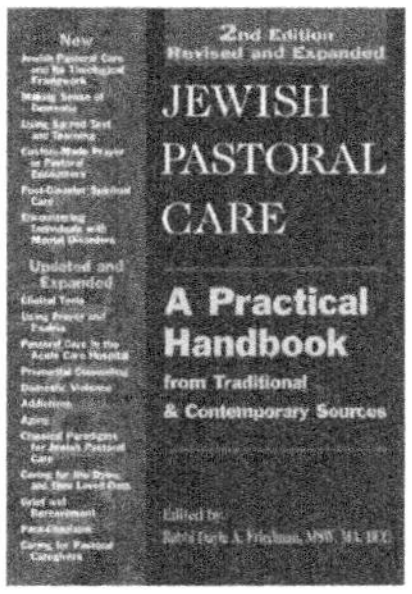

Jewish Pastoral Care, 2nd Edition

A Practical Handbook from Traditional & Contemporary Sources

Edited by Rabbi Dayle A. Friedman, MSW, MAJCS, BCC

The essential reference for rabbis, cantors and laypeople who are called to spiritually accompany those encountering joy, sorrow and change.

Back Cover Material

Growing Older Can Be a Time of Growing in Depth and Wisdom

"My sense is that the whole journey beyond midlife is a mysterious blend of light and dark, wholeness and fragility.... We have a chance beyond midlife to become the person we were truly meant to be. We can draw on everything we have experienced so far to contribute to the people around us and the wider world, and to find strength and resilience amid the challenges."

—from the Introduction

Whether you are fifty-five or seventy-five, approaching retirement or age one hundred, growing older brings remarkable opportunities but often also wrenching difficulties. Rabbi Dayle A. Friedman, a pioneer in reinventing and revaluing aging, mines ancient Jewish wisdom for values, tools and precedents to frame new callings and beginnings, shifting family roles, and experiences of illness and death.

For seekers of all faiths, for individuals and groups, for personal use and caregiving settings, Rabbi Friedman offers inspiration and guidance to help you make greater meaning and flourish amid the daunting challenges of aging.

***

"[This] is much more than a book that provides practical guidance and insights.... It is also a work of rare understanding, sensitivity, patience and kindness on the limitations of the human condition that will reward old and young alike."

—Rabbi David Ellenson, chancellor emeritus, Hebrew Union College–Jewish Institute of Religion

"[A] straightforward, clear-eyed, genuinely helpful guide for growing older.... Reading it is a pleasure and the message it delivers is potent medicine with a sweet aftertaste."

—Sylvia Boorstein, author, *Happiness Is an Inside Job: Practicing for a Joyful Life*

"A spiritual gem, filled with wisdom, a complex blend of realism and hopefulness. I know I will read this book again—perhaps many times—and will share it with people I love."

—Rabbi Amy Eilberg, author, *From Enemy to Friend: Jewish Wisdom and the Pursuit of Peace*

Printed in Great Britain
by Amazon

21697911R00140